CREATING CIVIL UNION:

Opening Hearts and Minds

CREATING CIVIL UNION:

Opening Hearts and Minds

Photographs and Essays

LINDA HOLLINGDALE

COMMON HUMANITY PRESS

October 2002
First Edition

Publisher's Cataloging-in-Publication Data

Hollingdale, Linda.
Creating civil union : opening hearts and minds / Linda Hollingdale.

p. cm.
LCCN 2002093435
ISBN 0-9722860-0-4
1. Same-sex marriage—Moral and ethical aspects—Vermont—Personal narratives. 2. Same-sex marriage—Law and legislation—Vermont—Personal narratives. 3. Gay couples—Legal status, laws, etc.—Vermont. 4. Gay couples—Vermont—Portraits. 5. Gay couples—Vermont—Personal narratives. I. Title.
HQ76.3.V47
306.84/8

Book and cover design by Barbara Hollingdale
Editing by David Weinstock and Ann Jones-Weinstock

Printed in the United States of America

This book may be ordered from the publisher

Common Humanity Press, LLC
P.O. Box 123
Hinesburg, Vermont 05461
www.commonhumanitypress.com

For Mary,
who opens my heart and mind daily

Contents

Contents

Acknowledgments

This project was created on a foundation of generosity. Many people, whom I call my angels, contributed in a number of ways to help make this book a reality. To all of you, I am truly grateful.

Thanks to Beth Robinson, whose enthusiastic, "You must do this project!" gave me the courage to begin; to Susan Murray for her constant and willing guidance in legal and business matters; to all of the people who agreed to participate in the project—your dedication astounds me. Dave Landers, my friend, is always first in line to support and nurture me. Mary Hurlie and Cheryl Gibson for years have given their resources, time, attention, and love in service to others.

My heartfelt appreciation to friends who did not hesitate to offer support for a project they believed in—Patricia House, Scottie Ginn and Pat Tivnan, Susan R. Jones, Mary Provencher and Ruth Uphold, Brooke Barss and Susan Wehry, Elise Brokaw and Nancy Yannett, Kym Boyman and Beth Robinson, Karen Hibbard and Susan Murray, Sally Fellows, Brookes Cowan and Cheryl Haller, Carey Kaplan and Andy Senesac, JB Barna, Mary Spicer and Tiffany Renaud, Helena Blair, Sonja and Maurice Pomainville, Ellie Wegner, Grace Kelly and Annie Brabazon, Joya Beattie, Fran Campbell and Dolly Fleming, Glen Gross, Laurie Wattles and Joan Carson, Laura Crain, Karen Pike; and thanks to the Kwini gals and guys who are living proof of deep friendship—your love gives me wings!

Saint Michael's College, my employer, gave me the valuable time needed to finish this book. David Weinstock and Ann Jones-Weinstock donated their time and talent to provide excellent editing—your directness and care made it easy. Bren Alvarez Farrington, top dog at Flynndog in Burlington, Vermont, joyfully said "Yes!" to my first gallery showing.

I am blessed to have grown up in an imaginative and generous family. My mother, Jackie, nurtured our creativity in our early years. By her example, I came to believe I could attempt anything. Alayne—my sister and sweet friend—your attentiveness, interest and support never cease to amaze me. Love and kisses to my precious nieces, Emily, Kate, and Hannah—you inspire me to keep growing!

A very special thank you to Barbara—my sister, friend, and book designer. Working alongside you on this project has been a gift I'll cherish forever. Your talents and heart are enormous.

And a final thank you to my love, spouse and soul mate, Mary Loney. In our wedding vows we proclaimed that we were one another's #1 fan; this project is indeed evidence of that statement. I am grateful beyond words for your love and support.

Introduction ~

During the spring of 2000, two independent questions came together to form an idea. What photographic challenge could I undertake to mark and celebrate my 30 years as a photographer? And, in relation to the work around civil union, how will I ever be able to tell my nieces (then ages 7 and 3) what it was really like? The combination of these two questions gave rise to this project, a photo/essay exhibit and book entitled *Creating Civil Union: Opening Hearts and Minds.*

With the assistance of Beth Robinson, one of the attorneys for the *Baker v. State of Vermont* lawsuit, an invitation-to-participate list was compiled. While the invitation could have been extended to hundreds, we deliberated and chose a group of people who represented a number of different roles and perspectives relating to the creation and/or support of Vermont's civil union law. My invitation asked each participant to share how they were personally touched and affected by their experiences during the process, and to be willing to have their photograph accompany their essays. Most of those invited said yes.

Ninety people are represented in the 47 photographs. It is my hope that these images will put a human face on a controversial issue. As you read the essays, you will notice similarity among many of the stories. I believe that these similar thoughts, emotions, and values are at the core of each participant's belief in equal rights for all citizens. You will also see diversity among the participants. Each person came to the process in a different way and integrated the experience in a unique manner.

While creating this book, I was touched by the power of the human spirit. People invited me into their homes, shared their personal memories, and discussed their hopes for the future. I felt blessed many times over. My heart was opened. I also became increasingly aware of the paradox of civil union. While it certainly is an unprecedented move toward inclusivity for gays and lesbians, it is a political remedy that keeps gay and lesbian couples as second-class citizens. My mind was opened.

However, even within the paradox, I continue to believe in the goodness of people. I know that seeing the humanness of another person is the first step toward improving relationships. As we continue to make room for one another in this world, it is my hope that this spirit of goodness will prevail.

This book celebrates that goodness and the amazing work of hundreds, which resulted in Vermont's historic legislation; it also serves as an invitation. I invite all readers to use the words and images within to help further open their minds and hearts to the realities of this latest civil rights movement, and to our common humanity.

Linda Hollingdale
August 2002

History and Terms ~

The following is an overview of the events leading up to the passage of Vermont's civil union law. A brief list of terms that may be helpful to the reader follows.

Between 1978 and 1999, several lawsuits were filed throughout the country in pursuit of same-sex marriage. None succeeded.

Baehr v. Miike (Hawaii 1999)

The "Hawaii case" had some early success in the courts. It was later dismissed due to a legislative ban on same-sex marriage that was passed before the Hawaii Supreme Court could hand down a favorable decision.

Baker v. State of Vermont (Vermont 1999)

- Three same-sex couples filed suit in Vermont on July 22, 1997 seeking the right to marry after they were denied marriage licenses from their respective towns.
- Vermont's attorney general, William Sorrell, requested that the court dismiss with prejudice all counts of plaintiffs' complaint directed against the State on November 10, 1997.
- Defendants' Motion to Dismiss is granted, and Plaintiffs' Motion for Judgment on the Pleadings is denied on December 19, 1997 by Linda Levitt, presiding judge.
- Appeals filed.
- The Vermont Supreme Court heard the oral arguments re *Baker v. State* on November 18, 1998.
- At approximately 11:00 a.m. local time on December 20, 1999, the Vermont Supreme Court issued its decision in re *Baker v. State.*

- The *Baker* decision

  "...We conclude that under the Common Benefits Clause of the Vermont Constitution, which, in pertinent part, reads, *'That government is, or ought to be, instituted for the common benefit, protection, and security of the people, nation, or community, and not for the particular emolument or advantage of any single person, family, or set of persons, who are a part only of that community...'* [Vt. Const., Ch. I, art 7.]

  ...plaintiffs may not be deprived of the statutory benefits and protections afforded persons of the opposite sex who choose to marry. We hold that the State is constitutionally required to extend to same-sex couples the common benefits and protections that flow from marriage under Vermont law. Whether this ultimately takes the form of inclusion within the marriage laws themselves or a parallel 'domestic partnership' system or some equivalent statutory alternative, rests with the Legislature. Whatever system is chosen, however, must conform with the constitutional imperative to afford all Vermonters the common benefit, protection, and security of the law...."

- Vermont's 2000 Legislative Session worked to remedy the mandate passed to them by the Vermont Supreme Court. This involved much committee testimony and two public hearings at the Statehouse during late January and early February.

- Vermont House of Representatives created "civil union" in lieu of granting full marriage benefits for same-sex couples. On April 25, 2000, H.847 passed in the House—after Senate amendments—by a vote of 79–68.

- Governor Howard Dean signed civil union into law on April 26, 2000.

- Civil union took effect on July 1, 2000.

Terms:

Baker case	(also *Baker* decision) *Baker v. State of Vermont,* the lawsuit that resulted in the civil union law (see above)
GLBT	Acronym for Gay Lesbian Bisexual Transgender (also, LGBT)
H.847	Civil union bill introduced in the Vermont House of Representatives
Hawaii case	*Baehr v. Miike,* the lawsuit filed in Hawaii in pursuit of same-sex marriage
PFLAG	Parents and Friends of Lesbians and Gays
VFMTF	Vermont Freedom to Marry Task Force

Beth Robinson ~

The struggle for same-sex couples in Vermont has been one of profound ambivalence and intense mixed emotions, from the beginning when we first started organizing in late 1995, and continuing through the present and, no doubt, beyond.

During the early days, I loved traveling around Vermont, meeting my fellow Vermonters, and talking about the reality of my life and the lives of so many gay and lesbian people. I was gratified by the number of people who might not otherwise have thought about this issue, or who may have even been skeptical, who listened thoughtfully and compassionately and came around. At the same time, I confess that a part of me resented that we had to work so hard to try to obtain the same basic legal protections and respect that most people take for granted. That part of me wanted to be home working in the garden.

Litigating the *Baker* case itself was an unqualified pleasure. I grew to intensely admire Holly and Lois, Stan and Peter, and Nina and Stacy, and their willingness to stand up publicly, declare their love for one another, and ask for a seat at the table. I grew to have the deepest respect and affection for Susan Murray and Mary Bonauto, co-counsel on the case, whose good humor and thoughtfulness made even the longest marathon telephone conference bearable.

The decision in the *Baker* case, however, caused me tremendous anguish. The Court's acknowledgment of our common humanity, and its rejection of the suggestion that there was any good reason to treat gay and lesbian citizens and our families as second-class, were truly inspiring. I have read a lot of decisions from a lot of courts in this country over the past decades, and I haven't seen many courts that have truly gotten it in that way.

At the same time, I was devastated by the Court's failure to live up to the lofty principles it articulated. Having recognized our right to a seat at the table, the Court then stepped back and suggested that perhaps we could be seated at a nearby table. After persuasively telling a story of inclusion, the Court turned around and suggested that something less than full inclusion might be just fine. The Court recognized that our claims were well grounded in Vermont's Constitution, a document which establishes a set of rights and protections that cannot be infringed by the vagaries of majoritarian politics. But then, rather than actually seeing its conclusion through, the Court took no action, sending us to the very political cauldron from which the Constitution is designed to shield unpopular minorities. Although I know in my head that *Baker* represented a step forward, I had hoped for and expected much better from this Court. December 20, 1999 was the most difficult day of my professional life.

The 2000 legislative session was mostly a blur for me. As with the Court, but to a much lesser degree, I was disappointed by the number of political leaders who knew better but were unwilling to stick their necks out in support of full equality for same-sex couples through inclusion in the marriage laws. At the same time, I was absolutely awed and inspired by the number of political leaders who put their political lives on the line to support civil union, a move which, in the end, subjected them to just as much antipathy as support of equality in marriage would have generated.

As the reality of the civil union law took hold, and the backlash continued with the approach of the November 2000 elections, I was deeply hurt and disturbed to see so many of my fellow Vermonters—including many otherwise good, hardworking, community-spirited people—allow their unfounded fears and insecurities to express themselves as hatred and animosity for gay and lesbian people. At the same time, I was positively heartened by the number of folks—often folks you might not expect—who stepped forward in solidarity with gay and lesbian people. Although we discovered foes we didn't realize we had, we also found welcoming shelter from the storm in many corners we might not have expected.

Finally, I was absolutely inspired by gay and lesbian Vermonters. Many lived in smaller communities and did not consider themselves to be activists. Many were not particularly "out." They did not necessarily choose this fight. Yet they heard the call and stepped forward to speak honestly and openly about the reality of their lives to their friends and neighbors, often at tremendous personal risk. In the sea of jumbled and contradictory emotions that I feel when I reflect on the last several years in Vermont, my admiration for and gratitude to these courageous souls float to the top.

Kym Boyman and Beth Robinson

Kym is a physician; Beth, an attorney at Langrock Sperry & Wool, served as co-counsel to the plaintiffs in *Baker v. State of Vermont.*

Reverend Brendan Hadash ~

The long journey toward equality for gays and lesbians began decades ago—before Baker *and civil union. While reflecting on the recent civil union endeavor, Reverend Brendan Hadash remembers the work in the earlier days of his activism.*

In July of 1984, the national gathering of Unitarian Universalists voted to make official church policy what was already commonplace: they became the first mainline denomination to support and encourage their ministers to perform "Holy Unions," gay and lesbian weddings. I have never been prouder of my church. My partner, Alan, and I immediately planned for our ceremony. On March 31, 1985, in West Burke, we were the first gay male couple in Vermont to have a wedding officially sanctioned by a denomination.

I never dreamed that one day we could make our relationship legal. We did everything we could to protect ourselves legally—wills, durable powers-of-attorney and so forth—but it was impossible to duplicate the rights and responsibilities of straight marriage.

In 1993, when I heard that the Hawaii Supreme Court had ruled in favor of the couples who had sued to obtain the right to marry, I got very excited. Perhaps one day gays and lesbians could legally marry in Vermont! I knew that we would have to start planning for the possibility. But how?

In 1995, in discussion with the Vermont Freedom to Marry Task Force, an idea developed. I would perform a public Holy Union at Pride Day in Burlington. This would raise awareness among gays and lesbians in Vermont. We found a couple, but when they backed out, I did a public wedding ceremony, similar to the one conducted

Reverend Brendan Hadash with Kate
in Glover, Vermont

at the 1993 Pride March in Washington, D.C., inviting any couple who wanted to be united anonymously to take part.

I had said for years that I was in the closet with the door open. If anyone wanted to ask, I would reply openly, but nobody had really asked. Then a reporter from the *Caledonian Record* called and wanted to do an interview with me about the ceremony planned for Pride Day. The Northeast Kingdom is the most conservative area of Vermont. Did I really want the fact that I was gay to be in the paper? I decided that I had to be true to myself and decided to do the interview. The result was a full page story with a large photo of me that appeared on May 31, 1995. The story had also been picked up by the Associated Press and appeared in various northeast papers. Luckily, the only negative responses I received were two letters from out of state. Locally, I got only positive responses, such as a surprising moment when an older woman approached me in the grocery store and offered congratulations.

At the ceremony itself, I was very nervous. Would gays and lesbians take it seriously? Would anyone disrupt the ceremony? I was relieved when it started to rain because only those who really wanted to be there stayed.

From where I stood, I could see two lesbians, dressed in white, who were reciting the vows after me. I could also see two men under an umbrella who were exchanging vows. Later I heard about a third couple with children, in the middle of a group of supporters, who also recited their vows. I suspect there were still others.

When the Vermont Freedom to Marry Task Force needed an *amicus* brief from religious leaders in Vermont supporting the right to marry, I accepted the project to organize VOWS (Vermont Organization for Weddings of the Same-gender). This organization eventually included 42 religious leaders, from six denominations, all willing to support same-gender marriage. The *amicus* brief was filed on March 6, 1998.

Of course, the creation of civil union is now history and I'm happy to say that I was able to make my own bit of history. On July 5, 2000, Alan and I were wed. I'm pretty sure that I am the first gay male minister to be legally wed in the United States.

Judy and Mike Olinick ~

As lifelong civil liberties advocates, we have always believed in full marriage rights for gay and lesbian couples. Blessed with many years of happy marriage and a wonderful family, we wished the same great joy for others, regardless of their sexual orientation. But we never dreamed that the first decisive step would be taken here in Vermont, or that we would have the privilege of participating in the process.

We were astounded by the speed with which same-sex marriage ceased to be an academic question and became a live and explosive issue. We wanted to help the effort in any way we could. We went to training sessions for supporters, made telephone calls and took shifts running the Freedom to Marry booth and tables at Addison County Field Days and the Ben & Jerry's Festival. We attended one of the legislative hearings in Montpelier, where we were not chosen to speak, and the statewide interactive TV hearings where Mike did get to make a statement. We wrote volumes of letters to the editors of local and statewide newspapers, responding to the unjust, often vicious attacks on same-sex unions and to the honest concerns of well-intentioned but apprehensive Vermonters.

We were greatly moved by the dedication, patience and persistence of civil union supporters we met, and by the struggles of same-sex couples and of parents who had been neutral or even hostile to homosexuals until, upon learning that their sons or daughters were gay or lesbian, they changed their thinking and reorganized their lives in order to support their children. We were enormously impressed and inspired by the brilliant and articulate leadership of attorneys Beth Robinson and Susan Murray, by the brave stand of friendly legislators and clergy, and by the sincerity and generosity of "ordinary people" who had never thought about civil union but slowly and courageously worked their way through the issues and became supporters.

Our own feelings about same-sex marriage and civil union never changed, but we learned to express them more clearly and succinctly, and to respond more calmly and effectively to the often unscrupulous tactics of the opposition. We experienced some of the old exhilaration and optimism we felt as college newspaper editors and as graduate students in the 1960s when we campaigned for civil rights and against the war in Vietnam. Our four children shared the excitement, many of our out-of-state friends followed the debate eagerly, and Judy's 90-year-old mother, after asking what civil union was, said with a laugh and a shrug, "Well, it's all right with me!"

We were overjoyed by the *Baker* decision, and ecstatic when the legislature passed the civil union bill. Yet we see what an extraordinary combination of circumstances led to this victory. The fortunate happenstance that no Vermont law defined marriage as an exclusively heterosexual union, the remarkable open-mindedness and unanimity of the State Supreme Court judges, and the prohibitive complexity of Vermont's constitutional amendment process, were all essential components of civil union's success. We fully appreciate this splendid coincidence; yet, because so many factors had to line up so precisely, we fear it may take years for other states to follow Vermont's lead in recognizing civil union. In the meantime, the regrouped forces of reaction will try, by every means possible, to reverse the legislative victory here, and to thwart a similar success in other states. The great challenge will be to hold the line against reaction and to win majority support for civil union here and throughout the country, so that turning back becomes unthinkable. In some ways, this may be a greater challenge than passage of the first civil union law.

But now there are many civil unions to celebrate and Mike, as a justice of the peace, has happily officiated at several. Each new ceremony helps to reinforce the truth that civil unions harm no one but help many wonderful couples, who in turn contribute to stability and social harmony in their communities. We, especially Judy, had begun to feel that one sad consequence of aging is a loss of belief in progress. But here, in beautiful Vermont, we have seen real progress, a true step forward toward justice and equality. We are grateful to have contributed, in however small a way, to this important new beginning.

We hope that we will soon see the day when civil union is called by its proper name—marriage—and is recognized and celebrated everywhere.

Mike and Judy Olinick, of Middlebury, Vermont,
volunteered at the Freedom to Marry Booth
at The Addison County Field Days.

Stan Baker and Peter Harrigan

When we were in the thick of the Freedom to Marry Lawsuit, later referred to as the "*Baker* case" or "*Baker* decision," reporters would often ask us, "Why did you decide to be plaintiffs in this case?" Our first answer was, "Because we fell in love." It is essential to remember that the Freedom to Marry Lawsuit that resulted in the landmark civil union legislation was first and foremost about love. For us, being joined in civil and holy union is, in its essence, an extension of our coming-out processes, being true to who we are in the eyes of God, and sharing that truth with our family, friends, and community.

Ultimately we decided that the other best reason to become part of the lawsuit was because we *could* do it—without losing our jobs, family, or friends. Both of our workplaces had non-discrimination clauses which included sexual orientation. Even so, we joined the lawsuit with caution, but without the overriding fear that many gay, lesbian and bisexual people confront every day. There were many couples, even here in Vermont, who would have lost their jobs, the support and love of their families, or their homes, if they had become plaintiffs. We have always felt that we were plaintiffs on behalf of all GLBT people in Vermont, in fact for *all* Vermonters.

One of the amazing parts of being plaintiffs in this case was having our commitment to each other become part of the public record. We were, for all intents and purposes, publicly engaged. This is not something that gay men and lesbians get to experience. Yet it is part and parcel of what non-gay couples enjoy routinely. Without giving it a second thought, heterosexual couples assume that they will be afforded the joy of sharing their engagement with their family and friends, of having it reported in the paper, and of having it fully recognized in legal marriage.

Stan Baker, a community development services clinical director, and Peter Harrigan, a college professor, at home in Shelburne, Vermont

Stan and Peter were plaintiffs in *Baker v. State of Vermont.*

Three stories come to mind from our experience in the lawsuit: our neighbor's reactions when the suit was first filed in July of 1997; what it was like for one of us to be *"Baker;"* and our family's reaction to our holy and civil union.

Our neighbor's reactions: On July 22, 1997 we came out to our neighbors in Vermont, all 650,000 of them, when our lawsuit was filed in Chittenden County Court, and our photograph appeared on the cover of nearly every newspaper in Vermont—*above* the fold. The reaction from our neighbors was immediate. One non-gay married couple brought us a bottle of champagne and a "Happy Engagement" card. They had stayed up most of the night talking about the issue, and come to support it and us, finding our family every bit as valid—and valuable—as their own. An elderly neighbor surprised us during breakfast. We were sitting at our kitchen counter when a small gray head came bobbing along just above the shrubs in front of our kitchen window. There was a knock on the screen door, and a voice cried out "I come in peace!" We opened the door and found Mrs. Cain in her housecoat. She had brought her copy of the newspaper—in case we wanted an extra—and had written, in black Magic Marker across the bottom, "Go for it!"

Stan's thoughts on being Baker: My name is Stan *"Baker."* During my lifetime, I have seen many changes based on courageous and controversial court decisions that resulted in increasing the rights of individuals or groups, such as the school desegregation case "Brown v. the Board of Education," and the first interracial marriage victory, called "Loving v. Virginia." I have also noticed that such cases are forever referred to by the name of the person who brought the case forward, even though the actual people had long since disappeared from the public eye. Today in Vermont, if you hear someone saying my name *"Baker,"* they are more than likely referring to the Freedom to Marry Lawsuit (July 1997), the Vermont Supreme Court decision (December 1999), or the Civil Union Legislation (April 2000). It still surprises me to hear someone talk about *"Baker"* when I am present.

Once, during the legislative debate on *"Baker,"* I was in the Vermont Statehouse, as Peter and I often were during the winter and spring of 2000. State Senator Elizabeth Ready took me by the hand and pulled me over to another legislator and said, "This is Baker!" It was a fun moment, but underlined for me that my name now has a life and meaning far beyond my own, bringing together my own individual identity and the case, the court decision, and the legislation, in a way that nothing else had.

Our families join together: We were, of course, anticipating our own legal joining and becoming a family in the true legal sense of the word. What neither of us had thought about was how powerful the joining of our two families would be. They all seemed to understand immediately that they were now legally joined as well. Peter's parents gave him away, and Stan's sister and brother-in-law gave him away, invoking the name, memory, and presence of his deceased parents. After participating in our ceremony, our two families quickly became friends—friendship built at first around shared caring about us but then, it was clear, on mutual interest and likes.

A week after our honeymoon, we were informed by Peter's mother that Stan's sister and brother-in-law were going to be visiting them in Maine and that his nephew was flying in from California to join them. They had embraced each other as family, never having met before our civil union ceremony. This coming together of our two families may seem insignificant to many, but if you have lived much of your life in secrecy, not expecting family to celebrate who you are as a person, much less honor your deepest love for another human being, this was a powerful and affirming moment for both of us. We now feel surrounded by the love of both of our families, our friends, our faith community, and our work colleagues.

We always try to remember, when all is said and done, "It's about love!"

Mary Bonauto

Along with Beth Robinson and Susan Murray, I was a lawyer for the plaintiffs in *Baker v. State of Vermont*. My work at Gay and Lesbian Defenders, a New England-wide legal organization combating discrimination based on sexual orientation, gender identity and HIV status, allowed me to work on several discrimination matters in Vermont over the years. The marriage case seemed like the next logical step to protect gay and lesbian Vermonters and their families. When Stan Baker and Peter Harrigan, Nina Beck and Stacy Jolles, and Lois Farnham and Holly Puterbaugh were denied marriage licenses solely because they were same-sex couples and for no other reason, we filed suit against the State.

Although it now sounds like a tired refrain, we were simply asking the Court for equal treatment under the law—something which is supposed to be a bedrock principle of our government, but which remains an unfulfilled promise to gay people. The promise will only be fulfilled when there are no privileged places from which any individual is excluded solely because of his or her gender or sexual orientation.

On December 20, 1999, the Vermont Supreme Court made its historic ruling that same-sex couples are entitled to the legal protections enjoyed by married people, but left to the legislature the details of how to implement that ruling. I think it's fair to say that our reactions that day were mixed. We saw the decision for what it was, a legal and cultural milestone that set a new benchmark for fairness. But on the other hand, by delegating to the legislature the task of implementing the ruling, it was a disappointment, especially since the court had the power—and I think duty—to order the simple remedy of ending discrimination with civil marriage. In past cases, challenging racial restrictions on marriage, the courts simply lifted the bans; they didn't send the matter out for legislative review.

Mary Bonauto is the civil rights director at Gay & Lesbian Advocates and Defenders (GLAD) in Boston, and served as co-counsel to the plaintiffs in *Baker v. State of Vermont.*

While the court did not do us any favors by thrusting us into the legislative arena, there was enormous good that came of the legislative and political processes. We had to make our case both to the members of the House and Senate, and to Vermonters generally. It is a good thing when people had to think about gay men and lesbians as parents, as partners, as neighbors and as part of the very same community they cherish. It's good because, over time, people realized that we have more in common than we have apart, and that differences are defined by the individuals rather than by sexual orientation *per se.* That means less fear, less demonization, less "otherness," and more understanding that people are people. That kind of thinking is precisely what the court decision propelled and the legislative process demanded, beautifully complementing the very same work already being done by the Vermont Freedom to Marry Task Force.

I was inspired by and admiring of my co-counsel in the *Baker* case, Beth Robinson and Susan Murray, and their law firm, Langrock Sperry & Wool. They did everything necessary to make sure we could present the case as completely and clearly as possible. I was honored to work with the plaintiffs, and humbled by their courage in coming forward in the lawsuit at a time of right-wing-fomented backlash against marriage for same-sex couples. Their plain-spokenness, their love for each other and their children, and their dedication to justice, were obvious to all.

I was awed by the many Vermonters who came forward both to the legislature and in their daily lives, to speak of their views of fairness, and of the gay and lesbian people and families they knew, and of past discriminations they and their loved ones had suffered.

I was grateful for each member of the House Judiciary Committee and Representative Tom Little's leadership of that Committee in facilitating a teach-in on civil and religious marriage in the United States and beyond.

I was refreshed by those members of the legislature who took the time to listen and to engage with lesbian and gay Vermonters in a way that they never had before. And, of course, I was moved to my core by those who cast their vote for civil union, because they knew the time had come to welcome gay and lesbian Vermonters openly in the law and our civic life, even when they believed—rightly or wrongly—that it would cost them their seats.

I was appreciative of our system of government, and how each branch played its role: the court declaring the constitutional rights of a minority; the legislature rising to that occasion—although it would have preferred otherwise—and developing a compromise attempting to meet the court's ruling; and the Governor, urging the completion of the process so that the law would be faithfully executed for all Vermonters.

I was excited and challenged by the contributions I could make: talking through the day's events or serving as a sounding board for Beth and Susan; persuading national gay and lesbian political groups that the best way to help was to continue letting Vermonters take the lead in this effort; trying to communicate to the gay community nationally about the historical moment at hand by writing email memos—to be forwarded all over the country; asking folks to call their friends and family in Vermont. Or in reviewing draft after draft of the civil union bill, thinking through what was entailed in creating a new kind of marital status never before seen in this country, suggesting language to add or delete, analyzing how to make the bill as comprehensive as possible, thinking through how to ensure that the civil union status would be portable from state-to-state. Or in reviewing every Vermont statute to ensure that every protection available to married people would be available to same-sex couples and their children. Or in getting the word out that people in other states could stand up for their families, too, pointing to Vermont as an example.

I was disappointed by the House Judiciary Committee's vote to proceed with civil union rather than marriage. Although I accepted the decision to proceed with the civil union approach, I believe the day will come when it is seen as an unequal and lesser status than marriage, and as a stepping stone to marriage. I believe that a number of legislators voted for civil union thinking that something less than marriage would blunt the vehement attacks by our opponents, but of course it did not. And I remain disappointed that some forces will work tirelessly to make sure that gay people are never accepted as part of the community in which we all live.

Overall, I was honored to play any role in the process, in which I was but one small actor among thousands. Civil union marks a turning point for the acceptance and legal respect of gay and lesbian families. We need that encouragement in what remains a long-term civil rights struggle—both in the courts and the court of public opinion.

Representative John Edwards ~

The morning was sunny and cold, the coffee soothing and hot. John Edwards looked through two very thick scrapbooks compiled by his wife as he remembered his involvement with the creation of Vermont's civil union law. Some letters were filled with hate and threatening words; these triggered John's painful memories. However, most of the scrapbooks' contents were messages of gratitude, encouragement, and accolade; these brought a look of pride and contentment to his face. Admitting that he could write a book about his experiences, he settled down to reflect on a few transformational moments.

I came to the issue because I was a legislator and more specifically a member of the House Judiciary Committee. I knew the issue of gay marriage was before the Supreme Court and I had not given it much thought. When the Court published the *Baker* decision in late December 1999, my initial reaction as a legislator was "Oh, shit."

My first personal reactions were that of a legislator who was interested in political self-preservation. I wanted to find a way to delay having the Judiciary Committee even take up the issue. However, I was informed that the Committee would make it the first and only order of business when we convened in January. From that point forward until the House had passed civil union, the pressure from constituents, fellow legislators, lobbyists, and the media was almost unbearable.

As chair of the Judiciary Committee, Representative Tom Little started a process of educating the Committee. We were a diverse group of five Democrats, five Republicans, and one Progressive. Over the years, we had developed a respect and trust for each other that would prove essential in getting us through to the end. I then read and reread Justice Amestoy's decision. Although I am not a lawyer, due to my background in law enforcement, I have a lot of experience in reading court decisions. It seemed to

John Edwards, of Swanton, Vermont, a retired state trooper and former state legislator, now works as a U.S. Marshall. He and his wife Deanna have six children and four grandchildren.

me that Justice Amestoy had framed the issues in two very compelling ways. First was the constitutional issue of equal treatment. The second was the issue of "our common humanity." For a long time I was in what I now look back on as my "denial and delay" phase. Basically I thought that the issues would be so complex that we could simply take testimony and stall the decision. In this scenario, we would run out of time and the issue could be put off until the following year.

However, as the Committee process continued, there were three turning points for me. First we heard testimony from many legal authorities from both sides of the issue. I paid particular attention to those who thought the Court had made a mistake. Their arguments in fact strengthened the basic premises that the Court articulated in the *Baker* decision. Secondly, we heard from many religious leaders. For me, they reinforced the constitutional concept of separation of church and state. Thirdly, the most compelling testimony came during the public hearings. I am in my late fifties and when I heard from people of my age, who had grown sons and daughters who were gay and lesbian, that struck a chord of realism that never left me.

At some point, I knew that the right thing to do was to fully support the *Baker* decision through appropriate legislation. I also knew that it most likely would mean the end of my legislative career. I had come to love serving in the legislature. I loved the process and the people and I thought I was a very effective legislator.

From the time the *Baker* decision was published, my life was full of anxiety. I really knew what the right thing to do was, but I had to screw up the courage to do it. In late February, after a morning of spirited committee debate, I found a very quiet place to sit and think. It was at this moment that I made the decision to support the civil union legislation. From that point on it was like a burden had been lifted from my shoulders. I fully understood what the probable consequences would be, but how often in life does one have the opportunity to make a real difference in peoples' lives?

Looking back on the experience, I did lose my seat in the legislature. As much as I loved the legislature, I gained more than I lost. The biggest thing I gained is the self-respect of knowing that I did the right thing. I feel sorry for some of my former colleagues who came up to me during the debate and said, "You did the right thing; I wish I had your courage." ❧

Representative Robert Kinsey ~

Robert Kinsey, from Craftsbury Common, was elected to Vermont's House of Representatives in 1970, and re-elected 14 times. However, in November 2000, Mr. Kinsey lost his job of 30 years. During the previous legislative session, Representative Kinsey, along with all of Vermont's legislators, had some difficult decisions to make.

I have always taken my legislative commitment seriously. At first I was upset with the Supreme Court decision in December. My job then became to ask questions. What does the Constitution say? Is the Supreme Court correct? If so, what do we do? So I read the decision and the Constitution. The Supreme Court was right in that all Vermonters shall be afforded the benefits and protections bestowed by the State. The next question was, is there discrimination? I find no greater proof of discrimination than all the amendments that were proposed and then defeated in the great debate on [civil union bill] H.847. Each amendment was telling these people, "Get back in your stall and shut up and be second class citizens." So the answer to my question is yes.

Bob Kinsey's conscience was formed by his experiences and his beliefs. He remembers the bigotry aimed at his Native American great-great grandmother, Roxie, and his great-grandmother, Bridget, an Irish immigrant. He is also haunted by a boyhood experience that shaped the man he is today.

In 1935 when I was eight, Sam Schneider and his wife were a Jewish couple with a small junk business near the Congregational Church in Barton. They were poor. I delivered a pint of milk to them every other day and got to know them. People made fun of them—a lot. Actually, what was going on in Barton back then was similar to what was going on at the same time in Nazi Germany, except we didn't shoot them or run over them with cars, but the hate was there. That same year, on Halloween night, I joined a crowd of young people up to mischief. One thing we did still haunts me today. The big boys found an old pail and filled it with muddy river water. Then they knocked real hard on Sam's front door. Now Sam had a choice. He could open the door and take that pail of muddy water in the face, or not open the door. But Sam knew that if he did not open the door, the crowd would get uglier and start smashing things to pressure him to respond.

Neither the police nor any neighbors would come to help. So Sam opened the door and took that pail of muddy water in the face. The crowd roared with laughter and went on their way.

Maybe Sam wished he wasn't different. Now, 65 years later, it is my turn to be Sam. Some of my constituents want to scold me for doing what I think is right—vote favorably for equal rights for all Vermonters. Like Sam, I will go—open the door and take that pail of muddy water.

Representative Kinsey voted in favor of civil union for lesbian and gay citizens. He provided the leadership he agreed to provide as an elected representative. My job was to help solve the problem. I voted my conscience. Yes, it cost me my seat. But I've had a 30-year career voting my conscience and many have thanked me for that.

Robert Everett Kinsey, of Craftsbury, Vermont is a farmer. He served as state legislator from 1970 to 2000, and as House Majority Leader from 1981 to 1985. He and his wife Eunice Rowell Kinsey have seven children and 17 grandchildren.

Carol E. Westing ~

The following letter was signed by ten justices of the peace from Westminster and Putney, Vermont, including Carol Westing.

> To the Vermont Legislature and Governor Howard Dean:
>
> We the undersigned Vermont Justices of the Peace hereby declare that we shall no longer perform any marriage until the State of Vermont recognizes civil unions between two persons of the same sex.
>
> As a matter of conscience, we are taking this position to uphold the Vermont tradition of equal treatment and respect for all. We are ready to perform civil unions as soon as the law permits.

The original idea had come from a minister in a neighboring town. When Carol considered the idea, she wondered about her responsibilities as a justice of the peace. Should I as a Justice of the Peace embrace this position, make a public pronouncement, and enlist the support of others justices in town? Would it make a difference or would it just expose me to negative reactions among my neighbors? I had been duly elected a JP by the towns-people, so did I have the right to refuse to perform one of my duties?

Her research revealed that performing marriages was indeed a discretionary act: a justice of the peace was not required to perform weddings. Carol and two Westminster JPs decided to take a stand. No weddings for anyone until civil unions were allowed. They crafted the letter, and began to pursue signatures. Of the nine other JPs in her hometown of Putney, five of them eagerly joined in the effort, while four indicated support for civil union, but not for this particular form

Carol Westing lives in Putney, Vermont
with Arthur, her husband of 46 years.
She has worked in education and is a
social and environmental activist.

of civil disobedience. The concerns of the four made me wonder if I was being a fool, but the eager, excited faces of the five who came to my house to sign the letter erased my doubts. We sent it to the local paper and to key figures in Montpelier.

Did this public act make any difference in passage of the civil union bill? Who knows, but it made a difference to me. Once I was able to perform my first civil union, I felt thankful that I had taken an active part in a movement that I believed in. I felt pride, too, in my state for its courageous, pioneering action.

To date, Carol has performed well over 100 civil union ceremonies. She and her husband Arthur have opened their home to many of these celebrations. Arthur and I feel the daily vibrations set off by those events that have filled our lives with a new meaning for love, devotion, dedication, and courage. The two of us knew that we had always had an intuitive sense of civil and other human rights, but now we have begun to more fully understand how demeaning it is to be denied those rights and the respect of others.

Carol recalls the summer day when her garden was filled with song, prayer, laughter, and tears. On that day she was honored to perform a ceremony for eight couples who joined together in their individual civil unions. She expresses her gratitude for being an integral part of this newly won freedom. We have been flooded with such overwhelming appreciation for simply opening our home to joyous celebration. There have been notes, pictures, gifts, and new friendships.

Like many people, Carol's and Arthur's lives have been enriched by their willingness to actively live their beliefs, to take a stand. And with more work ahead, their voices are still being heard. Wherever we travel now we talk about what Vermont has done and what we have experienced, in hopes that other people in other places will be inspired to work to provide the benefits of marriage to same-sex couples elsewhere.

Rabbi Joshua Chasan ~

In many ways, the courage issues around civil union were simply my courage issues. Going through the process, I grew more firm. Testifying in February felt like, "Now I can die because I have taken my stand." It was bigger than civil union. It was about personal integrity.

Joshua Chasan serves as rabbi of Ohavi Zedek Synagogue of Burlington—Vermont's oldest synagogue. As a Jew, I identify with the way that gay men and lesbians are stigmatized for being who they are, feared for how they love. It wasn't so long ago that the very nature of Jewish existence was called into question. I know that some Jews still fall prey to fear of homosexuality, even after what happened in Europe 60 years ago. It didn't matter then whether you were forced to wear a yellow star or a pink triangle. Either way you were considered less than human and not worthy of life.

Rabbi Chasan rejects the notion that one may "love the sinner while hating the sin." Many of the opponents of same-gender marriage are careful to distinguish between accepting homosexuals while rejecting homosexuality. But in this case, as with anti-Semitism, it is impossible to separate stigmatizing the sin from stigmatizing the sinner. The challenge for us in embracing same-gender marriage is to accept the very nature of homosexuality. Otherwise we are in danger of violating a Vermont citizen's right to be who he or she is.

As a Conservative Jew, his religious beliefs follow the Conservative Movement. The ancient rabbis themselves teach us to interpret Scripture, not to read Scripture literally. Scripture requires interpretation as moral standards evolve. For example, the Bible looks favorably on slavery. We don't. The Bible tells us to turn our rebellious children over to the state to be stoned. Rabbis were horrified by this command 2000 years ago.

Freedom of conscience is a given in both Judaism and Christianity. Scriptural interpretation is an ongoing responsibility.

Rabbi Chasan is aware that traditional marital arrangements were based on the biblical assumption of the subservience of women, and cites the recent lessons of feminism and other current thought as a source of expanded understanding. It is precisely my understanding of God's will, as it is shaped by the scientific, social, ethical, and psychological wisdom of our age, that leads me to recognize that we must expand our definition of marriage to include couples of the same gender. My reading of the Bible and Jewish tradition calls me very clearly to say that the love for each other of two people of the same gender has the same integrity and righteousness as the love of two people of different genders.

When gay men and lesbians want to affirm their commitment to each other, when they want to affirm the righteousness of their sexual relationship, far from sinning, they are helping to raise the moral standards of our society. What lowers moral standards is our robbing each other of the opportunity to live with liberty, each one of us free to pursue happiness in our own ways, as long as we do not infringe on the rights of others. Not everyone agrees about civil union. Not everyone has to agree. That's what our freedom is for—so that we can believe and think as we choose. But it gets dangerous when we lift up our own religious beliefs as the only political truth that's worthy of God's name.

I know many of my neighbors, members of my congregation, are struggling with the reality that gay and lesbian people want the same rights for their loving relationships as heterosexual people have. It wasn't too many years ago that I was fearful of homosexuality. Then I met real people who are gay and lesbian. I watched them parent their children. I saw them active in my synagogue and neighboring churches. I began to see how, for years, gay and lesbian people have taught our children, served as our physicians and nurses, lived as our neighbors. I don't underestimate the intensity of feelings about this issue. I have much respect for all Vermonters who are trying to sort through their feelings.

But, for homosexuals, still being beaten and murdered, the issue remains a matter of life and death. If we do not accept the integrity and righteousness of homosexuality by extending our understanding of marriage, we condemn gay men and lesbians to the risks of body and soul that are a consequence of our own difficulties in opening our hearts.

Rabbi Joshua S. Chasan of Burlington, Vermont,
on the *bimah* of Ohavi Zedek Synagogue

Rabbi Chasan finds profound clarity in simple truths. I don't know about you, but I know for myself that there are any number of ways in which my prejudices, the rigidity of my thinking, my own insecurities tempt me, certainly in the privacy of my mind, to rob others of their opportunity for life, liberty and the pursuit of happiness. I was educated by the justices of the Vermont Supreme Court. The eloquence of their decision, and their clear understanding that equity is only common sense, have helped me to understand the implications of what I know to be true: freedom is indivisible. My freedom is predicated on everyone else's freedom. If a gay man or lesbian is not free, I am not free.

At a time when so many of us are yearning for love in the world, I and many other religious leaders in Vermont cannot teach the love of God without affirming the love for each other and of Vermont couples who happen to be of the same gender. It would be futile anyway. King Solomon was wise enough to teach that "many waters cannot quench love." Love will have its way. Let us all come together to affirm that, whatever our views, love will have its way. ~

Sherry Corbin ～

Imagine living in a small town, a town in which you grew up. Imagine further what it might be like to be lesbian or gay while living in that town. Imagine trying to live true to yourself while keeping a constant vigilance over the reactions of neighbors, friends, and even family. Okay, you're doing pretty well and then a lawsuit unfolds in your state that represents one of the things you've always wished for—the right to marry the person you love. Change is in the air.

Sherry Corbin grew up and still lives in South Hero, a small island town in northern Vermont. In my adult years, I've been involved in town politics. I've been a fixture in the town hall for the past ten-plus years. I never hide my partner, Sue, and I don't think that there are many people in town who don't know we are a couple. In 1998, Sue and I had a big wedding that appeared to be the talk of the town. We could have sold tickets because there were so many people who wanted to attend. *However, Sherry's dad appeared to have a difficult time with the event.* We were out, but he wasn't.

Then in the summer of 1999, the Baker v. State of Vermont *lawsuit was being deliberated in the Vermont Supreme Court.* I was no longer working for the town, so I jumped when I heard that the Freedom to Marry Task Force was looking for a coordinator for Grand Isle County. Sue and I became involved, setting up Rotary meetings, arranging speaking engagements, sitting at the Task Force booth at local fairs, and motivating local supporters with a contingent of six other Islanders. We were really coming out. And still, my father seemed to be ignoring the fact that all this was happening around him.

The public hearings, the news coverage, the mailings, and other open expressions of opinion about the civil union bill brought new information to light. Points of view that had once existed right below the surface made their way to awareness. People whom I considered among my best friends were backing our incumbent representative who spoke and voted against the civil union bill. *One very hurtful reminder of this realization came in the form of political signs that began to appear all over town.* One day when I left for work I had three miles of no signs. But on the way home there were "Anti-Me" signs every 100 yards. It wasn't anti-civil union, it was anti-me. That was the worst. Not the language used, or the vehemence of the hatred, it was the signs.

During this time, another event occurred that triggered a major shift in attitude. A local man, someone I grew up with, took on the opposition of gay rights as his own private mission. He listed the names of civil union supporters from area towns, along with the Governor's name, on a document claiming that we all approved of the "sodomitic abuse of 14-year-old boys by 50-year-old men." He then posted this document on area churches and stores one Sunday morning. My father, who was treasurer of his church, arrived early to find his minister ranting over this letter. He then looked it over to find the names of both his daughters, Sue, his son-in-law, and his wife included on the list. He was outraged; this was no longer something he could ignore.

The community came together and held a candlelight march with over 250 people protesting the action. It moved people into a place of caring. They still may not have favored civil union, but now they cared and were open to listening. It seemed that once they decided to listen, their views were movable. And it seemed that my father became the father of a gay daughter and his interest level changed.

Well, the law passed. We happened to be in Italy when we read in an international paper that the House had passed the Senate version of the bill and the Governor was going to sign it into law. Later that summer, Sue and I had our civil union on the anniversary of our wedding. My dad came to this celebration also, but this time he had a big smile on his face and was enjoying himself. He never became that PFLAG kind of dad, but in his own way he is now "out" and okay with being there. He also loves his new legal daughter-in-law very much!

Sherry Corbin and Sue White with Lulu,
at their home in South Hero, Vermont

Sherry is an administrative technician;
Sue is an artist. They were joined in
civil union on September 6, 2000.

Lil Venner ~

Lil Venner was drawn into Vermont's civil union endeavor by her love for her daughter Karen. When Karen was born, I didn't know then how her birth would impact our family. I had the same dreams for her that other mothers have—education, marriage, family. I learned of her sexual orientation when she was a teenager, but I had no conception of the struggles that gay and lesbian teens go through as they lead their lives in a sometimes hostile society. Dr. Spock, my main resource, didn't include a chapter on this.

When Karen was in college, I heard a gay theologian describe the journey most gay and lesbian people take when they are aware of their orientation as adolescents. I cried for not knowing and not actively supporting her in her early years. I vowed at that point that I would be there for her, and perhaps make a difference for other gay and lesbian people. As a somewhat timid, stay-at-home mom, I didn't know where that decision would lead me.

Lil's decision certainly helped form the person she is today, and that person has most definitely made a difference in many lives. One of her most influential involvements has been with a national organization called PFLAG (Parents and Friends of Lesbians and Gays). She has provided support to Vermonters through PFLAG for years. Lil also worked for passage of the civil union bill. She recalls the many ups and downs of her own emotional journey.

I felt anger when people used distorted information and "research," as well as out-and-out lies, to describe my child and my gay and lesbian friends. I felt disbelief over the fact that supposedly intelligent people could be so ignorant, or so swayed by fear of the unknown. I felt joy when parents who had been "in the closet" came out and publicly supported their lesbian and gay children.

Lil Venner with her daughter Karen and Karen's three children: Liliana (6 months), Cole (3 years) and Taylor (6 years)

I felt barraged by the constant negative messages on television, radio talk shows, newspapers, bumper-stickers, day-in and day-out. It was hard enough for me, as a parent of a lesbian, but I wondered how gay or lesbian people themselves could maintain their emotional health. Particularly, I worried about gay and lesbian youth, or those questioning their orientation. I felt pride when lesbian and gay people stood up and told their stories, and when legislators voted their conscience knowing they would probably be voted out of office in the next election.

I felt sadness that, in a society facing so many critical issues, so much time, energy and money was spent on degrading and negating gay and lesbian families. I felt outrage when people from around the country stuck their noses into a Vermont debate. I felt elation on the day civil union became law, and the first time I heard a justice of the peace say, "By the power vested in me by the state of Vermont, I declare you joined in civil union."

Lil credits her strong spirituality as the source of her hope. She is proud of the manner in which the vast majority of supporters of civil union conducted themselves. We strove to be civil and not repay evil with evil. No matter how much garbage was thrown our way, our standards were not lowered. This made me proud to stand with the cause.

She also cherished the connection she had with folks along the way. After my two-minute testimony at the House hearing, I felt so inadequate, ineffective, and terrified. Then, as I left the House chamber, I was embraced and thanked by dozens of people. A few weeks later, when marching in Washington with the Freedom to Marry Task Force, tears and cheers greeted us along the entire route. I knew, deep within, that although I hadn't chosen to be in the struggle, I was supposed to be there: I was needed and I was not alone.

It was a combination of voices that worked together to get civil union passed. No one should underestimate their ability to make a difference. All who speak out speak not only for themselves, but for hundreds who can't speak. This is everyone's issue.

Brian Moore and Tom Robinson ~

"Coming Out" is not simply a phrase; it is an action statement. Gays and lesbians have always been faced with this challenge. Now, families and friends of gays and lesbians, along with the general population, have been invited to come out in an active way by supporting civil rights for lesbian and gay people. Vermont's struggle for same-sex marriage rights has pushed the coming-out process beyond previous limits. Brian Moore and Tom Robinson, a young gay couple, experienced their continual coming-out process in new and eye-opening ways through their work on the civil union legislation.

We first heard about the *Baker v. Vermont* case through two of the plaintiffs, Stan Baker and Peter Harrigan. Over dinner one night, we were excited to hear about the case, but at that point we didn't anticipate how, in a relatively short period of time, things would be different for all of us. Local groups supporting the Vermont Freedom to Marry Task Force began to form. Even though we weren't sure we had the time to give, a friend talked us into attending a volunteer meeting. The people we met were amazing. Everyone had a lot of passion and energy. There was no way we couldn't be a part of this. By the time the meeting was over, we had already signed up for many different committees and projects.

One of the most important volunteer tasks was education. Discomfort around homosexuality is widespread, and much of the discomfort is based on myths and misinformation about lesbians and gays. Education and truth-telling would be the key to expanding the general public's understanding of the issues. This job would need the courageous coming-out effort of gays, lesbians, and their allies. We were happy to see so many non-gays joining the volunteer cause. Even though civil union didn't affect them directly, they were just as passionate. It was ironic to hear the opponents of civil union say that it would rip the state apart. We saw just the opposite. We saw people coming together, sharing their stories, and showing the strengths of our community. We connected with people—gay, straight, or other—while working for civil union, and we made many friendships.

We created bumper stickers, made posters, and walked door-to-door with our information. Our favorite campaign involved asking people at an outdoor mall in Burlington to fill out ready-made Valentine cards. These cards were then sent to state representatives asking them to pass same-sex marriage. The reactions of passers-by were so mixed—some were happy, some glared with contempt, and some didn't care either way.

Among the most powerful experiences during the campaign were the two public standing-room-only forums held at the Vermont Statehouse. Brian recalls, the Statehouse was mobbed with Vermonters both for and against same-sex marriage. Before the hearing started, I was volunteering at one of the main doors, passing out bright pink stickers to people as they arrived. The stickers read: I SUPPORT THE FREEDOM TO MARRY. The stickers were intended to brighten up the House chamber and let the representatives know how many in the crowd supported same-sex marriage. Our opponents were doing the same. Their white stickers read: GOD'S LAW—ONE MAN, ONE WOMAN. Why did our opponents feel so threatened by same-sex marriage? Realizing that they didn't even know me, I felt sorry for those who opposed our rights.

When civil union finally became law, Tom and Brian faced a relationship decision. Before the whole civil union issue, we had thought about having a commitment ceremony but we weren't sure what we would do. After spending so many hours fighting for the legislation, we both came to the decision that we needed to have a ceremony to celebrate. The debate over civil union showed us why marriage is so important, not just for the couple but for the community. Our ceremony included over 150 people. It was amazing to have the love and support of our family and friends. We made each guest at our wedding a witness to our commitment. Everyone present at the wedding signed his or her name on a document which contained our vows. It now hangs in our living room where we pass by it daily.

Civil union will have an impact for years to come. The children who grow up seeing civil union in Vermont will see same-sex couples as normal as heterosexual couples. They will eventually ask, "Why the distinction?" Marriage is inevitable. We won't settle for anything less.

Brian Moore and Tom Robinson
in Colchester, Vermont

Christ Church Presbyterian ～

Margaret Mead said, "Never underestimate the power of a small group of committed citizens to change the world. Indeed, it has never been done otherwise." One example is the membership of Christ Church Presbyterian (CCP) in Burlington, Vermont. The collective energy and commitment of this congregation to do the work to create change is remarkable. CCP folks most definitely "walk the talk" of social and spiritual activism.

CCP is one of a few "More Light" Presbyterian Churches in the United States. This means that CCP not only welcomes GLBT individuals, they celebrate and embrace their presence. For years, this congregation has been working with the larger Presbytery to officially recognize and accept its partnered gay and lesbian deacons, elders, and ministers. It was not surprising therefore to find several members of CCP at the center of the fight for same-sex marriage.

The decision to become constant and fierce supporters was not made without struggle. The people who chose to fight for the rights of their gay neighbors had already made their own journey of awareness. Ken Wolvington recalls: In 1984, when CCP was declaring itself a More Light Church, I was not among the leaders in making that decision. I probably wasn't out-and-out homophobic, but I was, at best, ambivalent about the church's stand regarding GLBTs. I was, after all, born and raised in a culture that was very homophobic and I well remember that in my earlier years, queers were…well…queer! It wasn't until I had the opportunity in 1988 to get to know a gay person well enough to put a face on homosexuality. That changed my perspective radically. Gay rights became a justice issue for me.

Ken's wife Jean recalls a similar shift. At first I was uncomfortable with gay people, and then I heard a young woman speak in church about what is was like to be a nine-year-old girl who was different. That was when a light appeared for me. As I learned

Members of Christ Church Presbyterian

Front row (l to r): Glen Gross, attorney and co-coordinator for Vermonters for Civil Unions; Jean Wolvington, educator and volunteer; Reverends Rebecca Strader and Michael Brown, co-pastors, wife and husband, of CCP;
Back row (l to r): Ken Wolvington, retired from G.E. and volunteer; Barbara W. Emerson, retired nurse and volunteer; Doug Taylor, management consultant and co-coordinator for Vermonters for Civil Unions

more, and met more people, I had to be involved; I had to fight tooth and nail for inclusiveness in the church. For me it was a challenge to emphasize humanity: God doesn't make mistakes.

Doug Taylor believes his roots of involvement started in the mid 1960s. He describes more conservative, limited views on civil rights and politics in his early years. But his discomfort with those ideologies also motivated him: I changed my political compass 180 degrees. In 1993, I discovered CCP and their More Light Mission. Through that exposure, I became aware of the daily discrimination against the GLBT community. Here was something that really touched a chord! This was an issue that fit my newfound political-social outlook. I think I instinctively recognized that this was fundamentally the same struggle that I sat out in my younger years, and I was determined that I was not going to allow an opportunity to stand up for human dignity pass me by again.

Oftentimes, during the weeks of struggle, opponents would speak of their discomfort with homosexuality and then use that feeling as a defense for their continued opposition. While that is an option, one used quite frequently in this world, the truly courageous option involves using one's discomfort as an invitation to learn. People at CCP are adept at choosing the courageous route. This was clearly evident throughout the civil union endeavor.

This "small group of committed citizens" spent hundreds of hours attending hearings, giving testimony, writing letters, making phone calls, canvassing neighborhoods, registering voters, marching, offering financial support, and encouraging others to move through their discomfort into a place of truth and reality. They reached out with inner strength to talk with their friends and colleagues. They shared a version of God's message that differed from the version used to judge and condemn lesbian and gay people, a message that reminds us to love our neighbors as ourselves.

This challenge is simple, yet it takes thoughtfulness and hard work as Doug Taylor discovered. Let's face it, I, like many other white, straight males, am a recovering racist, a recovering homophobe, and a recovering sexist. I think this experience really brought home a glimmer of what it must be like to live as a gay person in a mostly straight world where you never know when or where the next homophobic word or action will come at you. Like civil rights, this battle will never be over. There will always be people who are bigoted and hatefully homophobic, just like there are people after 30 or 40 years who are still racists.

Everyone is welcomed at God's table...YES!

For the most part, however, I am really hopeful. I see that the vast number of folks really understand that this is not a moral issue or a question of a lifestyle choice, but a matter of people having the right to be who they are, and happy and free in doing just that!

CCP's Reverend Becky Strader states the simple truth: Our congregation wouldn't be the same without our gay and lesbian members and their families; I can't imagine CCP without them, and frankly, I *don't* imagine it. ❧

Joseph and Marilyn Watson ❧

"*Mom, Dad…I'm gay." This basic message is proclaimed in a number of different ways by children throughout the world on a daily basis. Parents, and other family members, receive information about their child that changes the way they have viewed and understood that child.* About ten years ago our son, Joseph, age 28, came and shared with us that he was gay. He knew that accepting this knowledge would be difficult for us. We belonged to a very conservative church that thought being gay was a sin. However, we knew our son's integrity and assured him that we loved him unconditionally. *Joseph and Marilyn were faced with the decision on how to incorporate this news into their lives. They chose positive action.*

We began to read, we attended meetings at Castleton College to learn about homosexuality. We got support from PFLAG; they provided material and answered our many questions, and over the intervening years we have been able to provide the same support to other parents. *By taking personal responsibility for their own coming-out process, Marilyn and Joseph increased their own awareness and understanding while ensuring an open and honest place in their son's life.*

This connection contributed to the Watsons' happiness when Joseph met Michael, who became his life partner. Joseph and Marilyn were touched by the union ceremony Joseph and Michael held in 1993, and they watched as the two men took all the possible legal contract steps to secure the mutual reciprocal benefits they would need in their life together. When their son became involved in the Freedom to Marry Task Force and asked them to take part in a video presentation he was producing for the Public Access TV station, they said yes to their first activist endeavor.

At first it was very stressful for us to take part in the civil union movement, but we wanted the best life for our son and his partner. We attended the hearings in Montpelier, staffed the Freedom to Marry booth at the Vermont State Fair, spoke at civic club meetings, and participated in panel discussions.

Almost all of the experiences have been positive. It has been amazing to us that so many of our friends and relatives, as well as those we meet in our travels, have been so supportive of the Vermont civil union stand. It is not just the young people but older people who have no problem with civil unions and say that they are long overdue.

As for the continuing challenges, the Watsons seemed fueled by their passions. We get angry with people who are trying to impose their personal religious philosophy by means of law on us and our gay and lesbian friends. The blatant falsehoods published by the opposition to civil union and the selective interpretation of the Bible give true testimony to the agenda of the conservative right.

As the work continues Marilyn and Joseph look forward. It is our hope that the process of fairness for all people will spread to all of these United States as it is doing in some enlightened countries of Europe where same-sex marriage is becoming legal. ~

Joseph E. and Marilyn J. Watson at home
in Rutland, Vermont, along with
their son Joseph F. Watson

Nina Beck and Stacy Jolles ~

We had been together as a couple for about two years when we decided that we wanted to be married, to publicly voice our love and commitment for each other in the presence of our families and our community.

We were married in a traditionally Jewish wedding ceremony on March 22, 1992. Our vows spoke of honoring each other as individuals, while sharing the passages of life together. We spoke of wanting to make this spiritual union a legal reality, but such a possibility seemed vague and distant even with the Hawaii case pending.

When we heard of the Vermont Freedom to Marry Task Force, we were excited about a movement advocating for legal change. We became part of the *Baker v. State of Vermont* case because we wanted to provide the legal protections of civil marriage for each other and mostly for our children, Noah and Seth.

Noah was eighteen months old when we became involved in the lawsuit. But the day the lawsuit was filed, July 27, 1997, Noah was in the hospital fighting for his life. Noah did not survive. His brother Seth was born two and a half years later, and he was exactly one month old on the day of the Supreme Court decision, December 20, 1999.

We have come to accept civil union as a compromise. We know that it is a huge step forward in civil rights for gay and lesbian people, and we also see that it is a "separate and not entirely equal" solution. We continue to work for and hope for the day when same-gender unions will be given full legal recognition. ~

Stacy Jolles and Nina Beck, of South Burlington Vermont, were plaintiffs in *Baker v. State of Vermont.*

They're shown here with their sons Seth (seated on Nina's lap) and Noah (behind them in photographs).

Mark Emmons and Hal Parker ~

At our civil union, our delightful 13-year-old daughter /stepdaughter, Kappes, read a poem about families and what that meant to her. She talked about how her "multiple families" have changed her life and who she is because of the many worlds of which she is a part. Her view of the world is open, tolerant and accepting. We are thankful for this view, because we live in the Northeast Kingdom, the most conservative part of the state. In the heat of the civil union struggle, she observed hate, fear and injustice first-hand—in the form of death threats and hate mail we received. We considered moving away, but a family motto was created: "It takes more courage to stay." She has enormous courage, a quality that will help see her through life.

For us, the civil union process has been about making a huge positive change in the world with our personal power. Exhilaration overcame the fear. When our minister pronounced, "By the power vested in me by the state of Vermont, I now pronounce you spouses joined in civil union," we knew we were making history, and our new family was to be acknowledged.

After the reception, which was really a victory celebration, it was time to get back to living life in the Kingdom. Our new family has had many reactions from the community. Many of our blood family members will not contact us. Several old friends dropped us from their lives. A grocery store clerk will not speak to us. And when we're at a concert or school event, there is shunning or "the look." We also connected with people we never considered would be supportive; we made new friends. As a family, we talk about this often and let it be. We work hard to surround ourselves with positive, loving, non-judgmental people—our "chosen family."

Hal Parker, Mark Emmons, and Kappes Emmons
of Derby, Vermont

Hal is a training consultant, church musician, and former flight-attendant. Mark is an elementary educator, church board member, political activist, and gardener. Kappes is a high school honor student, band member, and X-country ski team member.

Surrounded by chosen family, it helps us to remember what is important: love, laughter, learning and spirituality. We are committed to teaching Kappes that fighting for fundamental rights and responsibilities is the right thing to do.

To others who may have the opportunity to work for the rights of all people, we say, "Go for it!" and help make the world a better place. ❧

Senator Jim Leddy ~

"The Path to Civil Unions: A Legislator's Journey," a seven-page essay written by Senator Leddy, chronicles some of the events from 1998 to 2002 that he found memorable and influential. His words reveal a thoughtful and level-headed view on the political processes involved; however, what clearly stands out in Jim's reflections is his compassion for other people and his dedication to the values of family, faith, and empathy. He recalls the struggles and the blessings.

For me personally, it has been very difficult because I live in the community where I was born and raised and grew up. It is difficult and painful to be accused of betraying your values, of betraying your faith, of betraying your parents and your family and your heritage. In all of the communications, the letters, the phone calls, the emails and the face-to-face contacts, there have been very strong and very heartfelt opinions offered on both sides. However, sometime in late March [2000], I received a letter which proved to be a touchstone in the entire civil union journey because it touched the core value of my position. It was from a Williston woman, Helena Blair.

> Dear Senator Leddy,
>
> I am writing to you as a 78-year-old Catholic mother of eight. This letter is not about statistics or biblical interpretation. Instead, it is about a large Williston farm family and a son who 26 years ago announced that he was gay. What were we to do? Understand instantly or cast him aside? Accept him in a patronizing way or continue to love him unconditionally? We brought up all eight children with the same value system, but one was gay. Did we do something wrong? Surely our son would not choose societal, political, emotional, and possible physical persecution,

> but then, he didn't choose. He knew, and we know, that he was just plain born gay. I can say that God blessed us with eight children, and my God made no mistake when he created homosexuals and when he gave us our gay son. Please support the civil union bill.
>
> Sincerely,
> Helena Blair

I have four children, and on this issue, my wife and I are at peace with our four children. If one or more of my children were to come to their mother and me and say that they were gay or lesbian, our love and our acceptance would be unconditional, and I pray it would be as loving and accepting as Helena Blair and her family's. And if that child were to come back the next week or the next year and say, "I'd like you to meet the person that I love, that I have committed to and that I wish to spend my life with," that same unconditional love, I hope and pray, would be there not only for our child, but for the person they had chosen. And if I believe this for my children, I must believe it for the children of others.

Much has been said about the issues of saving traditional marriage and of the threat to marriage by the Court decision and this bill. I can only speak for myself and for my wife of 28 years, and say, no matter what struggles we've had during the past 28 years, and no matter what challenges we will face today, tomorrow and in the years to come, there is nothing in this court decision, there is nothing in this bill, there is nothing in the committed relationship between two people of the same gender that presents a threat to my marriage. I believe my marriage is traditional. I believe it is sacred, and I believe it is a sacrament, and nothing we see here today presents a challenge or threat to any of what I believe and hold true.

Jim's Catholic faith holds a central place in his life. He derives comfort and strength from his relationship with God. He was deeply troubled by the vicious verbal attacks on gays and lesbians and on his fellow legislators, especially those that came from church leaders. He approached leaders in the Republican Party, urging them to denounce such tactics, but to no avail.

He finally wrote a letter to his bishop asking him to speak out against the hate: "...As a legislator who voted for the civil union law, I am fully prepared to be accountable for my vote on this and many other issues, and if that means I lose, then democracy will have spoken. But I am not prepared to sit silently and allow such hate and bigotry to spew forth unchallenged from the bully pulpit, for while we do not need fewer pulpits, we

Jim Leddy of South Burlington, Vermont, is a state senator. He served for 20 years as executive director of the Howard Center for Human Services before retiring in 2000. He and his wife Clorinda Marro Leddy have four children: Sarah, Giovanna, Brennan, and Seamas.

Her message...I have come to understand that homosexuality is just as real as heterosexuality, that no one makes a choice and that each person is a unique and very special human being worthy of respect and honor.

Her message to those who had the power of a vote...I believe that to vote on issues involving civil rights for the 10% of our population who do not have the political strength of the remaining 90% requires a vote from the heart—from one's very soul. And once the mind and heart are free of fear and past prejudices, it is easier to cast the vote, to thereby gain respect and a clear conscience.

Her message to the clergy...May I humbly ask you—Have you ever really known or communicated with a gay person? Have you ever watched the kindness and thoughtfulness that they seem to exemplify? Have you ever wondered, over the years, as you faced your congregation, which tenth person sitting in a pew or on the altar, was a homosexual? And have you ever hurt inside, even a little bit, when in the name of Christ Himself, you may have judged or condemned those whom Jesus Himself neither judged nor condemned?

How have Vermonters received Helena's messages? It's hard to know, however it's safe to guess that many opportunities to think more openly were created by her words and deeds.

Senator Jim Leddy brought Helena Blair to Vermont's attention when he responded to a hateful remark made at a local informational meeting by citing a moving letter from Helena. After Leddy's comments, there was dead silence...Surely no one knew who I was, not even Jim Leddy, so after getting approval to speak, I simply said, "I'm Helena Blair." The standing ovation that followed so overwhelmed me that all I could do was cry. I am forever thankful to Senator Leddy for sharing my message.

This moment marked the beginning of a remarkable relationship between Helena Blair and the hundreds of Vermonters who are nourished by her actions. What continues to be amazing is Helena's humility. Other than raising my family, never in my lifetime have I ever felt like I gave so little and received so much in return. I shall be forever grateful for having had the opportunity to be a part of the most historically important human rights legislation ever to be passed in the State of Vermont. May this love and understanding we have come to know continue on to be a part of who we all are.

Helena Blair lives with her family in Williston, Vermont. She has been involved as a political activist for the past several decades. Her son, Lawrence Blair, lives in Boston, Massachusetts.

Jakki Flanagan ~

Often, in moments of tremendous change, corresponding invitations for transformation appear. In June 2000, Jakki Flanagan accepted the position of grassroots organizer for the new political action committee, Vermonters for Civil Unions. This position grew out of the volunteer work she had been doing for the Freedom to Marry Task Force during the 2000 legislative session. The campaign rocked my world. I never worked so hard in my life, never was so emotionally invested in any job or cause…or maybe even any person, except my daughter, in my life. It was the most excruciatingly difficult and rewarding job I ever had.

Jakki remembers many amazing moments in the course of doing this work. The most prominent was canvassing, the act of knocking on doors to talk to people about civil union. We did this in the more "hostile" areas of the state; after all, we didn't need to preach to the choir. It was painfully intimidating, and for me, equally rewarding. We would go to each door, individually—so as not to overwhelm anyone. As I stood there, I wondered, during that miniature eternity before the door opened, if the person behind it would slam the door in my face, yell at me, do something worse, or be supportive.

As hard as it was, canvassing taught me how important individual conversations are. I had surprisingly many conversations with people, who identified themselves in the beginning as strongly anti-civil union, but which ended on a much more moderate, even supportive, note. I do not credit my powers of persuasion. Rather, I believe the people I talked to who changed their stance probably never had a conversation with someone who was supportive of LGBT rights. In fact, they often stated they didn't know or had never met anyone who was gay.

Jakki Flanagan and Morgan Flanagan-Folcarelli

Jakki is a grassroots organizer.
She and Morgan live in Hinesburg, Vermont.

When reading through the list of rights that accompanied civil union, it was standard to ask people which ones they felt gay couples should not have. As we checked off the choices, frequently they'd say, "Well, they should have that one…and well, they should have that one too…of course that one…." Many times, as the list was completed, they'd say something like, "Well, I just never thought of it that way before." One conversation in particular with a 92-year-old woman was along those lines. In the end, she said, "Funny…I guess I do support civil union after all, but I don't know how I can help, I'm 92 and the only thing I do is play bridge." I lightly suggested she could have this same conversation with her bridge partners, to which she responded, "You know what, I think I will…I can do that." Then she shook my hand, quite solidly, and thanked me for having this conversation with her.

Another conversation was with a woman in her mid-20s, who said in no way did she support civil union. She felt it was discriminatory because, "You know, my boyfriend and I can't get one…." So we then had the conversation about marriage, and that we'd prefer to have marriage, not civil union, but we couldn't get that passed in the legislature. Her response was, "Ohhh, well then, I think it should be marriage, not civil union, that gay couples get."

Not all the positive interactions were with women. There were men who were more positive by the end of a discussion as well. One conversation with an older man who identified himself as anti-civil union, took place over his fence. Quite literally, we were on opposite sides. I leaned on the fence from his front yard, he from his back. At the end of the conversation, he said "Well…this isn't really about marriage, this is about people's rights. We here in Vermont kinda mind our own business, you know. These folks need these rights, so I guess I support it."

Jakki's visits with complete strangers opened not only doors, but also hearts and minds. The work, she remembers, made me laugh, made me cry, and made me believe in the incredible goodness of people.

Along with her political growth and the growth she encouraged in others, Jakki experienced a personal transformation as well. My life changed in ways I never could have predicted. Though married, I realized I had feelings, deep feelings for another woman. So, I found myself living the campaign, involved in a marriage in crisis on its own merits, and now having feelings for someone that I could not share.

Jakki followed her awareness, worked through the end of her marriage, cared for her young daughter, and poured her remaining energies into Vermonters for Civil Unions. Time has passed and I've since met the most incredible woman. I never knew, never could have imagined, there would be someone who shares my spirit in such an essential way. My seven-year-old daughter, Morgan, loves and adores her as well. Seeing the two of them together, watching, listening to them interact, a feeling of awe overwhelms me, inspired by the blessings in my life. I am grateful for having discovered the honesty, and beauty, of my true self.

Reverend Gary Kowalski ~

I tend to be a traditionalist. I grew up attending church almost every Sunday. I got married when I was studying for the ministry at Harvard and will soon be celebrating my twentieth wedding anniversary. Being the father of two beautiful children is one of the greatest blessings of my life. I rejoice in family values.

That's why I've long believed that the benefits of matrimony should be available to all. In 1997, I asked the governing board of my congregation at the First Unitarian Universalist Society of Burlington, to bring a resolution to our annual meeting endorsing the concept of same-gender marriage. The resolution passed unanimously, and we became one of a handful of churches and synagogues to sign on as *amicus* in the case then pending before the Vermont Supreme Court.

Testifying to the House Judiciary Committee in Montpelier, reading a letter that has been endorsed by clergy of many denominations, including bishops of the Methodist and Episcopal churches in Vermont, helped me put the furor in perspective. Opponents of civil union, I noticed, almost always framed their arguments in terms of injunctions, ordinances and prohibitions. Their tone was legalistic. Supporters, on the other hand, spoke of relationships, like one mother saddened that her homosexual daughter would never be able to have the kind of celebration that her two sisters had so much enjoyed. One side seemed to operate out of a love of rules; the other embraced the rule of love.

When a homophobic letter was mailed to every household in the state warning of the dangers of same-sex union, my nine-year-old son and I painted a big, rainbow-hued poster announcing "We Support Freedom To Marry" and placed it in the signboard on

From left to right: Reverend Gary Kowalski, Holly Jones, Dori Jones, and Noah Kowalski display their hand-crafted sign at the First Unitarian Universalist Society of Burlington, Vermont.

our church lawn, prominently facing Church Street. When the sign was vandalized, we put it right back up.

In a sermon I delivered on the topic, I likened myself to the character Tevye in *Fiddler on the Roof.* Living in the little town of Anatevka, Tevye's life is anchored in the immemorial customs of Jewish life. Without tradition, Tevye acknowledges, the world would be as unbalanced and precarious as a fiddler on the roof. But then Tevye's world is turned upside down, as one by one his daughters decide to marry outside the norms.

Not so long ago, in our grandparents' generation, many lived in villages like Anatevka, where marriages were arranged by the local matchmaker, where a daughter would never dream of marrying without her papa's consent. Interfaith marriages were frowned upon. Thankfully, much has changed.

But some things have remained the same. In one of the most touching scenes from the musical, Tevye asks his wife, "Do you love me?" And Golde's reply strikes a chord of truth, "For 25 years I've washed your clothes, cooked your meals, cleaned your house, given you children, milked the cow. For 25 years I've lived with you, fought with you, starved with you. Twenty-five years my bed is yours. If that's not love, what is?"

Golde seems to be saying that the bond between two people who have shared all the vicissitudes of life is so deep that even the word "love" seems inadequate. It is a reality firmer and more lasting than any mere mood or emotion. It is an unqualified devotion to each other that entails both tenderness and tribulation. It comes from washing the dishes and quarreling over who will dry. It comes from taking turns feeding the cat and standing together crying over the grave when that dear old house cat finally grows old and dies. It comes with that softening born of age and experience, when after so many years together, your partner has never looked so beautiful....It comes from still being able to laugh, after everything the two of you have endured.

That visceral, vital bond is what marriage is all about. The Vermont Supreme Court's decision affirming "equal rights" acknowledges that all of us—gay, straight or none of the above—share in a timeless human longing for commitment and companionship. Marriage is a tradition that has evolved through the centuries, but through many permutations has served to enrich and humanize life. Both church and state should do everything possible to sanction and encourage such long-term, faithful partnerships.

To the legislation establishing civil union, I can only respond with a hearty "Amen." Or as Tevye might say, "L'Chaim!"

Lois Farnham and Holly Puterbaugh ∾

Holly and Lois, two of the plaintiffs in the Baker *case, recall the difficulties associated with the civil union journey; yet, they also realize—with gratitude—the blessings.*

Are we glad we did it? You bet! Did we think it was going to be such a nerve-wracking, stress-filled process? No. Would we do it again? Probably.

Ten years ago we would have said, "You're crazy!" if you suggested we would end up doing what we did. It was difficult to go anywhere and not be recognized by folks. We did not want to become poster children, but ended up being so. We don't think anyone thought it would be quite as stressful as it turned out to be.

As far as the emotional toll, you name the emotion, we experienced it. We were on cloud nine; we were at rock bottom. We were happy, then disappointed and sad. We were scared, hurt, exhausted. We were frightened at times, wondering what might happen to us, or to our family. We were ecstatic over people's support—from some unexpected places. We were disappointed that some relatives refused to acknowledge and discuss such an important event. We were angry about some reactions of intolerance and ignorance.

Yet, blessings came out of this. People talked openly about civil union. The news media was forced to discuss it. The legislators investigated it and realized how many people this issue did impact. So many were affected, especially after people like Fred Phelps [antihomosexual protester from Topeka, Kansas] came to town. There was major media attention—*Good Morning America, the BBC, USA Today.* We, and the realities of same-sex couples, became more visible.

We also learned quite a bit. We learned that it is much better to be open and honest. We could be honest with ourselves and not worry about who knew what. We believe we both grew during this process and talked more openly about things. We learned about the care and support of most of our co-workers and some of our relatives. We learned about the tremendous intellect of our attorneys. And we learned that almost every individual has a relative, friend, or acquaintance who is gay or lesbian. We became more tolerant of others and their differences.

What would compel two women to step out of the relative peace and quiet of their shared life to live in the spotlight of a major public event for several years? Younger people—those in their twenties—telling us that we were their role models. You see, others had gone before us and we decided it was time for us to take a stand. More people needed to see that there are gays and lesbians among them and maybe they just didn't know it. People needed to see that gays and lesbians lead normal lives, not unlike theirs. We both are educators and believe that education is needed around these issues.

In the end, what did we gain? Our civil union, almost equality, public acceptance and recognition, more honest images of ourselves and others, and more gray hair! ~

Holly Puterbaugh and Lois Farnham,
plaintiffs in *Baker v. State of Vermont*

Holly teaches math at the University of Vermont and Lois
is a school nurse supervisor in Essex Junction, Vermont.
They live in South Burlington, Vermont.

Clare A. Buckley

I am honored to have worked as a lobbyist for the Vermont Freedom to Marry Action Committee, starting in January 2000, shortly after the Vermont Supreme Court issued the *Baker* decision. Working with Beth Robinson, Susan Murray, Mary Bonauto, Dorothy Mammen, and fellow lobbyists at Kimbell Sherman Ellis, including Steve Kimbell and Bryan Mills, among others, along with thousands of gay and lesbian Vermonters and allies to get the civil union law passed, was the most rewarding lobbying job I've ever had.

So much took place in that four-month period from January to April 2000, it is hard to know where to start. Here are a few high and low points that stand out for me.

It was incredible to watch legislators—many of whom never thought much about gays and lesbians never mind them marrying—struggle with how to vote. One legislator said to me early on, "So they want to get married?" It simply never entered his mind. He ended up voting for civil unions.

These legislators didn't ask to be on the cutting edge of the gay rights movement in the United States, but as a result of the *Baker* case they were. They rose to the challenge and showed great courage. Some were harassed and threatened. Others lost their seats over their vote. When I get cynical about politics, I remember this.

The thing that was the hardest for me was the hate. At the public hearings, in the letters to the editor, in paid newspaper ads, in the testimony before the committees, by all the out-of-state groups and individuals who came to Vermont to oppose the bill, hate came nonstop, from all directions. There was a lot of fear. As a woman, I have felt

Clare Buckley works as a lobbyist for Kimbell Sherman Ellis in Montpelier, Vermont.

discrimination, but nothing like this before. Ironically, it was this hate which some legislators later told me, led them, in part, to vote for civil union.

In contrast to the hate, gay and lesbian Vermonters opened up their lives in a very public way, to let everyone see who they were, and that there wasn't anything to fear. I recall at the first public hearing, a lesbian from Norwich, Vermont, came out before the whole state of Vermont when she testified about how a civil union type law would benefit her partner and children. The next day her picture was plastered on the front page of a statewide newspaper. This woman and the thousands of others like her who contacted their legislators or otherwise spoke out were the true lobbyists for civil union.

The two public hearings held at the Statehouse were an important turning point in the debate. Hundreds of people packed every inch of the well of the House, even with a raging snowstorm outside one night. While a select few legislators, who sat on the House and Senate Judiciary Committees, heard lengthy testimony on topics ranging from the history of marriage to how other countries such as France and the Netherlands have legally recognized same-sex couples, it was the public hearings that exposed most legislators to the arguments on both sides. The public hearings, which were broadcast live on the radio, provided Vermonters with the opportunity to climb the same learning curve as their legislators. These hearings were critical to public awareness and acceptance of what ultimately became the civil union law.

Another high point was when the civil union bill passed its first vote in the Vermont House on March 15, 2000. The Statehouse was like a three-ring circus that night. There were hundreds of supporters on the Statehouse steps who came to rally in support of the vote and were being serenaded by Tammy Fletcher singing, "This little light of mine, I'm going to let it shine." In the Senate chamber "Farmer's Night" was under way, with a Civil War theme—folks dressed in Civil War garb, with a drum corps band. With this backdrop, after debating the civil union bill all day, the House took its first vote on the bill.

The vote in the House was close, and there were enough legislators who wouldn't say how they intended to vote, that no one truly knew if the bill was going to pass. Most of the supporters who attended the rally couldn't fit in the House chamber and were listening outside the chamber on a loud speaker. Immediately after the Speaker of the House read the vote indicating the bill had passed preliminary approval, those in the chamber remained silent, but the supporters outside the chamber erupted in this spontaneous, loud cheer of sheer joy. It is a sound I'll never forget.

Opening the newspaper on July 2, 2000, and reading a story about the first couple to enter into a civil union was unreal—as if I never actually expected a couple to get a civil union. Up until that point it was solely a legal and political battle. Looking at the picture of the two women in Brattleboro signing their civil union license made it all come alive. There are few jobs that are so gratifying. I feel blessed to have been involved with this effort and to have caught a glimpse of history in the making.

Bari Shamas

Historically our society has asked those in the minority, those who are different from most, to limit themselves in order to ease the discomfort of the majority. "Why do you have to flaunt it?" "Just don't push it in my face." "What you do in your bedroom is your own business." The message is, "Stay away, stay hidden, keep it to yourself, act more like us..."

Bari Shamas had "opened hearts and minds" in her work for the Vermont Freedom to Marry Task Force, reaching out to the public. But in the private realm, within her own extended family, there was still work to be done. In an exchange of letters with her cousin Maxine, a British woman living in Italy, Bari explained why gays and lesbians fight for the right to live openly as full equals in society.

Dear Max,

I can really appreciate your desire to disregard labels. When I lived in Amsterdam in 1979, people asked me if I was a lesbian. At that time, I had no sexual experience with women but was open to the possibility. However, I saw no need for labels. Even after moving back to Brattleboro and becoming intimately involved with a woman, I was resistant to using the label. Now, to be truly honest with myself and others, I do use the term, because I am a lesbian.

I am a lesbian because by living with and loving Diane, we are a family. However, we are treated as less than a family by laws everywhere but in Vermont. Before civil union was available, we created every legal document possible to protect ourselves and our relationship with our two children, Raphi and Irene. But they only safeguarded us in certain limited circumstances.

Diane and Bari Shamas with their children,
Irene and Raphi in Putney, Vermont

Heterosexuals have privileges that they are not even aware of. In the state of Vermont there are over 300 laws that support spouses; federally, there are over 1,000. Heterosexual couples can choose to forego marriage. Queers who want to buck the system and turn up their noses at the institution of marriage don't really have that option. Until there is the choice to be legally married, there is no choice in not getting married.

Beyond the legal support is societal acceptance. I believe that the lack of legal support for gays and lesbians, legitimizes society's homophobic and discriminatory ways. Although at Raphi and Irene's school, they do not have a problem with name-calling or peers being hostile because their parents are two moms, it is very common in schools that words like "queer," "fag," "dyke," "sissy" and other such slurs are used to put fellow students down. To a great degree that taunting is accepted. In workplaces across our great nation it is still OK to discriminate based on sexual orientation. So many people do not have the luxury and safety of being out or honest with themselves and others. I don't know the exact numbers, but hatred of gays or lesbians is on the list of top motivators in violent crimes, right up there with race and ethnicity. Gay teens are also more likely to commit suicide than their peers.

My mother-in-law was worried about our traveling in Italy. She knows that it is a Catholic country and is worried for our safety, because we are not good at disguising our relationship. We don't make out in public, but we use terms of endearment, and function as a couple and as parents. In that way our relationship is obvious to anyone with half an eye open. This is a concern she would not have if one of us were the opposite sex.

In many ways our family looks like yours, but I am sure that, by the fact that we are two women living together, there are differences. We do not live by gender roles defined by the heterosexual paradigm. We do not make assumptions that come with living in a majority population. Nor do we expect that people live by a narrow definition of acceptable behavior.

You asked, "Do you call me a hetero, a straight or what?" I call you my cousin Maxine, and to further describe you, I'll tell other people that you are British and living in Italy. As to your sexual orientation or preference, I would not presume to say. You have chosen not to define yourself that way and I respect that. Just because someone is married to a person of the opposite sex does not mean that they are straight. Lots of people move from such marriages to relationships with someone of their own sex. Or some have an arrangement with their spouse to carry on extramarital same-gender relationships. Lesbians also move into relationships with men (we lovingly call them "hasbians"). Then there are transgender people who legally are one gender but in their hearts, minds, and physical appearances, feel and act as the other sex. I know there are lots of possibilities.

When you wrote about a friend who was trying to adopt children with another person, I suspect that most straight people would have assumed that she was in a relationship with a man. But I did not. Maybe you ask, what does it matter? Well, for gays and lesbians, adoptions are often filled with additional landmines. Most states and many countries forbid adoptions to gays and lesbians. I know lots of couples who hide their relationships when doing paperwork and meeting with social workers because they want to adopt from these countries or in those states. For them, there is an added burden of having to hide a beautiful aspect of their family. That is not only sad but something that I can relate to as a lesbian; it is a shared experience.

I am grateful for your acceptance of me as I am and understand your desire not to label. I don't get the same kind of acceptance you offer from everyone in my family. Last spring when my folks were vacationing with us in Florida, my mother said to me, "If I had my life to do over, I would dedicate it to curing and eradicating homosexuality." I know my mother has uncomfortable feelings about my life and that took some of the shock away from her declaration, but it stung and surprised me still.

Lastly, I am proud of our life, what we have done and continue to do. I believe that our experiences will nurture and benefit not only us, but our kids and everyone who is open enough to see the beauty that is here.

Love, Bari

Working for the right to marry taught Bari that her story can invite change. It was that work, opening one heart and one mind at a time, that she found most rewarding.

Beth Diamond and Craig Bingham

Have you walked a mile in someone else's shoes? This question was a key motivating force in the decision many non-gay people made to become involved in the struggle for same-sex marriage. As they worked in support for the civil union bill, Beth Diamond and Craig Bingham found themselves putting on those shoes on a regular basis. Their courage helped to transform their understanding of discrimination and the need to continue the work for change.

Beth: I didn't come out of the womb knowing all about civil rights. Although I grew up in a diverse, cosmopolitan area of New Jersey and have had friends who were gay, lesbian, and even transvestite since high school, it didn't mean that I automatically got it when the issue came to the forefront in Vermont. However, when our church, Champlain Valley Unitarian Universalist Society, was becoming a "Welcoming Congregation," I began to understand the kind of discrimination gays and lesbians have always had to deal with. And by the time the public hearings started in Montpelier, I think I truly understood, at least as much as a heterosexual person can.

Craig: When Beth and I fell in love, we wanted to be united in every way possible—that's why we chose marriage. I knew many gay and lesbian couples who felt the same way about each other as we did, but didn't have that choice. I felt compelled to join in the Freedom to Marry movement because I clearly saw it as a matter of civil rights. I had been too young to work for civil rights in the sixties, but today civil rights for gay and lesbian couples is a social justice issue that resonates with me. Working for the Vermont Freedom to Marry Task Force (VFMTF) has been a wonderful growth experience for us. Beth and I have had our eyes opened to the prejudices that we ourselves carry around every day.

Craig Bingham and Beth Diamond of East Middlebury, Vermont, at the Champlain Valley Unitarian Universalist Society of Middlebury

Beth: Working in the VFMTF booths at county fairs raised our consciousness. One day, at the Addison County Fair and Field Days, a rather large middle-aged man with short hair, dressed in green work clothes approached. We both tensed in anticipation of being harassed. We were surprised when he told us that he and his partner had been together for 30 years! He made a large donation and bought the video of the oral arguments before the Vermont Supreme Court. After he left, we admitted that we had judged him by his appearance. This was a lesson we were to learn more than once.

Craig: People made assumptions about us as well. We were often looked at with puzzled expressions. Was Beth a man in drag? We are a pretty openly affectionate couple, and some folks couldn't quite figure it out! More than once we were asked why a heterosexual couple would be staffing this booth. When we explained that we wanted our gay and lesbian friends to be able to have all the rights and benefits that we did, sometimes we could perceive a shift in people's thinking.

Beth: I was lucky enough to have my name selected to speak in Montpelier at the first hearing where the Joint House and Senate Judiciary Committees took testimony from the general public. I had not prepared anything in advance and didn't realize how intimidating it would feel to sit at the end of that long table. I thought that my heart would beat out of my chest, and I don't know how I was able to speak, but I did. I expressed how important our marriage was to Craig and me, and that I was ashamed to have rights that some of my friends did not have. I ended by saying that I was proud to be living in Vermont, that I was proud of the Supreme Court of Vermont and that I wanted to be proud of the legislature, too.

Beth and Craig: One of the most incredible moments was to be in the House Judiciary Committee room when the civil union bill was voted out of committee. Many people aren't aware that if a vote had been taken at the opening of the legislative session, civil union would have been defeated in committee by a vote of 8–3. But after hearing testimony of literally hundreds of people, including ministers, rabbis, psychologists, social workers, representatives of Vermont's Tax Department, the Vermont Secretary of State, and lots of ordinary folk, the Committee's final vote was in favor 10–1...and the one dissenting legislator was holding out for full marriage benefits! This, to us, was a real miracle—the miracle of transformation through education.

To put oneself in a position of vulnerability and discomfort in order to effect change is the sign of a true ally. Beth and Craig, in a spirit of generosity and compassion, believe that the rights available to them ought to be available to all.

David Moats ~

Seated in front of a small group of college students, staff, and faculty, David Moats discusses, with an air of humility, his experiences during Vermont's same-sex marriage deliberations. Although soft-spoken and seemingly shy during this conversation, his recollections are filled with a tone of purpose, courage, and confidence. While he stated he is not fond of getting people mad at him, he was clear that he, and his newspaper the Rutland Herald, *supported gay marriage. His goal was to do the job of providing a message that was both timely and helpful.*

He is now famous for winning the 2001 Pulitzer Prize for Editorial Writing for several of his editorials related to civil union. His even-handed, thought-provoking messages provided moments of clarity and respite in the churning waters of public opinion during the debates.

His editorials encouraged people to understand the humanity of their opponents by reminding readers that it is possible to understand, without necessarily agreeing with, the other points of view. This editorial, which appeared in the the Rutland Herald *on February 9, 2000, is one of David's favorites:*

A charitable view

The House Judiciary Committee heard moving testimony last week from one of the lawyers who brought the suit that led to the Supreme Court's decision requiring the state to provide equal benefits to gay and lesbian couples.

The lawyer, Susan Murray, described the pain of people who must listen to frequent and repeated public denunciations of their morality and character. "It's really painful to hear people say, 'You're immoral. You're an abomination,'" Murray said.

Gay and lesbian Vermonters have heard a full range of denunciation in the past several weeks. It is something they have heard all their lives, beginning with common school yard taunts and culminating in the passionate condemnations heard at the two public hearings inside the State House.

Murray used the words of Episcopal Bishop Mary Adelia McLeod in saying, "Gays and lesbians are the only group that are still politically correct to kick."

Sometimes, the attacks on gays are plainly mean-spirited and oblivious to the pain they cause. In some cases an unholy mix of anger and fear suffuse the language of those who condemn gays and lesbians as immoral. These attacks are the equivalent of the fire hoses and police dogs that were turned on civil rights workers in the South in an earlier day. They are a reminder that seeking justice exacts a price.

But opposition to same-sex marriage or domestic partnerships comes in many shadings, and it is useful to distinguish those who hate from those whose opposition has other origins.

Bishop Kenneth Angell has prompted resentment in asserting the Roman Catholic opposition to same-sex marriage. It's helpful, however, to realize that the Catholic position arises, not from bigotry, but from a specific teaching about sexuality, a teaching that a lot of people have difficulty with, including millions of Catholics.

It is the Catholic teaching that sex is a gift meant for the purposes of procreation and that sex indulged in for other reasons is a misuse of that gift. Thus, sex outside of marriage is not condoned. Even sex within marriage when the possibility of procreation has been blocked by birth control is not condoned. Gay sex, in this view, does not fall into the category of permissible sex.

It is possible to disagree with this view while still recognizing it to be a legitimate doctrine of a major religion aimed at providing guidance in the chaotic realm of human sexuality. It may offer some comfort to supporters of same-sex marriage to see through to the humanity of the opposition and to recognize the reasons for opposition are not always founded in bigotry.

At the same time, opponents of same-sex marriage have an obligation to see through to the humanity of a vulnerable minority. Anyone tempted to condemn homosexuality as other than normal ought to consider that it is quite normal that within our population 5 to 10 percent—the number is not important—happen to be gay or lesbian. For each of us, it is normal to be who we are, whether we are heterosexual or homosexual. It has always been that way, and the sooner we recognize it the better.

David Moats of Middlebury, Vermont is the editorial page editor for the *Rutland Herald.* He is a journalist, playwright, and father of three.

There are among us already those eager to sharpen the swords of conflict on the issue of same-sex marriage.

But the people of Vermont are in this together. Opponents and supporters of the Supreme Court's ruling are part of the same community, and as the discussion moves forward it is important to cultivate a charitable view of those on the other side. That way, however the issue is resolved, Vermont will be a better place in the end. ❧

Representative Marion Milne

The Supreme Court was bold in deciding that couples of the same-sex ought to enjoy equal benefits, but it gave the assignment of making it law to the legislature. That's what the legislature does. The court wanted us to do it. So, right before Christmas [1999], the court issued its decision, handing this duty to the legislature. Nothing has been the same since...not in the Statehouse, not at every coffee shop, and not at every kitchen table throughout the state.

I recently reread the *Baker* decision. It's inspiring. The court looked at our Vermont Constitution and tried to understand the meaning of the words, "government is... instituted for the common benefit, protection, and security of the people...and not for the...advantage of any...set of men..." That section is the heart of the Constitution. It is the expression of our democracy. It is based on a policy of inclusion. It says no one gets special advantages because of who they are.

The very public process of passing this idea of civil union into law was also a private journey for each legislator. This legislation wasn't something I ever expected to have to take a position on. I am not a politician. I am a mother, a grandmother, a wife, a neighbor, a friend. I started a travel business in Barre. I raised my family in Washington, Vermont, and then I went to college and graduated when I was 40. I served as a trustee of the library for many years, and I first ran for the legislature when I was 60.

I tried to understand whatever was before us for a vote. Every day was something new. It always demanded my full attention and study, but that year it asked something more. Deciding how to vote on civil union was not easy. I listened to anyone who had something to say about it. I spent a lot of time just thinking about it.

I thought about how hard it is to be different in this world. All of us are different in some way; none of us has escaped the hurt of being criticized for our differences. Whether it's because you're short or tall, because you're a girl, because you have a funny accent, or because you want to wear your hair a certain way, we all know what it is to be excluded. It seems right that law should treat everyone equally.

Imagine how it feels to be gay in a small Vermont town. It's either a secret or something everybody talks about. Some disapprove and are open to showing those feelings. Some are fearful, some accepting. Should the rights of gays and lesbians be respected? For me, that wasn't a hard question to answer.

The Vermont legislature had already made it a crime to treat gays and lesbians differently in public accommodations, employment, adoption of children, and government services a few years ago. But this time the question was different. It was whether gay and lesbian couples in a committed relationship should enjoy the same benefits as married couples.

For legislators, there was a special pressure. You can imagine how it feels to have everyone want to give you advice, or at least share an opinion on this issue. And there were far more than two opinions on this legislation. Some were for it because the Supreme Court told the legislature it had to act. Some were against it because it didn't go far enough. Some wanted benefits for any two people who had formed any caring and faithful relationship and would sign an agreement together. Some wanted us to defy the Supreme Court and the Constitution and do nothing. Some thought it was simply a good idea even without having a mandate from the Court. Some thought it was sinful and morally wrong.

I talked to dozens of people about the idea of civil union and about the *Baker* decision. What I heard was very disturbing. I was moved by the stories I heard about what it is like to be gay or lesbian in Vermont, about discrimination and fear, and the real consequences of intolerance.

I turned to my family for support. I talked with my husband and children. I thought about my grandchildren, and the kind of society I want for them. I admit I thought a little bit about what might happen to my chances of re-election, but that did not dissuade me. I spoke out. I did what I thought was right. I tried to find words to express what I felt in my heart. I voted for the bill and I have never regretted that decision. I am proud of that vote.

Marion Milne in her office
surrounded by photos of her family

She served in the Vermont House of Representatives
from 1994 to 2000. Marion and her husband Donald
have lived in Washington, Vermont for over 40 years.
They have three children and eight grandchildren.

Our State Supreme Court has ruled that same-gender partnerships should receive the same benefits as marriages between men and women. The objective of this ruling is to achieve equal treatment under the law for same-gender couples. Experience tells me that when we attempt to place into separate categories of definitions groups which the law attempts to place in the same category of treatment, one group will be favored over the other.

When I was a child, my family was escorted from one passenger car of a southbound train to another. We were separated from the accommodations we had chosen because white passengers who boarded the train after us could not tolerate sharing the same space with us. The accommodations were the same, the seats were just as comfortable, and the view was just as scenic. However, we did not feel as though we were treated equally as the other passengers.

The issue concerning same-gender marriage involves matters of civil rights, because they concern heterosexual couples learning how to share the same space and category of fair treatment with same-gender couples. This is clearly a civil rights matter, and, as an African American, I have learned that "separate but equal" is not equal. In 1954, our nation's Supreme Court ruled that any attempt to divide the races in public schools would result in unequal education. This ruling attempted to correct previous assumptions that black and white children could receive the same quality education in segregated schools. Evidence shows that when people are segregated from one another, their thoughts, behavior and outlook will favor those with whom they are most familiar, while they will treat with suspicion, mistrust and hatred those who are different from them. This is apparent by the fact that up until the very recent past, interracial marriages were outlawed in many parts of our country.

Given the glaring fact that this nation has made damaging prejudicial distinctions in so-called "separate but equal" education and in interracial marriages, we cannot assume that by extending rights and benefits to same-gender couples that are enjoyed by different-gender couples, especially under a different name, they will actually receive them. The ruling of the State Supreme Court does not reflect a heightened level of public tolerance toward homosexuals. Bigotry and harassment are still daily experiences they endure. Affording same-gender covenanted relationships the legal benefits and title of marriage is a matter of civil rights, because this sort of legislation would protect these couples from the bias and bigoted perceptions, manipulations and persecutions of others. But the more basic reason same-gender marriages should be supported is

Reverend Dr. Arnold Isidore Thomas in his office at the United Church of Christ in Burlington, Vermont.

that, by my own experience, these are couples whose commitment, affection and love for one another, and whose devotion to members of their family, are as strong and exemplary as many heterosexual marriages.

As far as same-gender marriages blessed by the church, I would say, again from my experience, that these are relationships founded and strengthened in love. The Bible says that: "Love is from God, and everyone who loves is born of God and knows God… God is love, and those who abide in love abide in God, and God abides in them." (1 John 4:7, 16) Firmly believing this, I would add: "Those whom God has joined together, let no one separate." (Matthew 19:6) ∾

Laura Davidson and Nora Skolnick

The process of working for civil union accelerated our coming-out process in our community and family. This was an issue that was too important for us to sit back in our own little world up in the woods and watch from the sidelines. We knew that it was critical to join the effort and help bring a dream into reality. Our involvement was gradual, starting with reading emails and editorials and proceeding to writing letters and attending rallies. When the House of Representatives held hearings at the Statehouse, we, along with many other gay and lesbian Vermonters, had to make the very scary decision whether or not to speak publicly about this incredibly personal part of our lives.

The more we listened to the opposition, the more galvanized we became. Each attack on same-sex couples felt like an attack on us personally. Each and every "Take Back Vermont" sign and hateful letter to the editor hurt and frightened us deeply, but they ultimately served to make us more determined to speak out and show people that we were here, we were not going away, and that we had the right to be treated equally.

When the Senate hearings were held regionally at Vermont Interactive Television sites around the state, we were the only two pro same-sex marriage supporters present at the Orange County location at the time the lottery for speaking occurred, so were both chosen for the hot seat. We can still feel the lumps in our throats and apprehension to realize, not only would we be speaking in public in front of neighbors and co-workers who were actively opposing us, but our stance on the issue would be circulated around the state on radio and television. The local newspaper was covering the event as well. Sure enough, in the next issue of the paper, there was our picture on the front page! It was one more step in our coming-out process in the community.

These coming-out steps continued with speaking on call-in radio programs, and culminating, for us at least, in having our picture in *Time Magazine.* All in all, it's a great story. Laura met a freelance photographer who was covering the Supreme Court session at the Vermont Law School where she works. They discussed the upcoming candlelight rally planned for later that evening and the fact that they would both be attending. He asked if he could photograph us, but Laura declined, saying we still had some reservations. We discussed it on the drive up to Montpelier that evening and decided to go for it if anyone asked us. Of course someone did, and once that person started shooting, we spotted the individual from earlier that day and gave him permission as well. We stood next to each other and went as far as even hugging each other in the bitter cold while the cameras clicked and flashed around us. For a few minutes we were a bit like deer frozen in the headlights of the *paparazzi*. Once the commotion ceased and we thought everyone had finished, we turned to each other and smiled, out of relief and self congratulations at our newly found courage. We then gave each other a short peck of a kiss on the lips. Ah, the innocence of such a moment!

Late one evening less than a week later, nearby neighbors called to let us know that there was a photo of us in *Time Magazine.* That itself was a surprise, but they upped the anxiety-ante by informing us that we were kissing in the photo! After rushing down the road to see the photo ourselves, we promptly telephoned our parents and siblings to relay the news and let them know that, although the photo wasn't really all that big and we were not identified in it, we were certainly recognizable. It was and still is gratifying that the reactions of our parents, friends, and co-workers ranged from hugs of support and "Don't worry" to yelps of glee and "How great!" Although our five minutes of fame were more than enough for each of us, we now proudly display a framed copy of the photograph in our home. As we said earlier, it's a great story!

Once the civil union law was passed our coming-out process continued. Planning our wedding ceremony was a major event which even a year earlier we didn't imagine. We were in love and planning a wedding! Neither of us wanted to keep the preparation of the celebration of our commitment and love a secret. Heterosexual couples talk about their weddings and we wanted to as well. The reaction from most people was gratifying. The hug from a boss, the excitement of seeing friends and family who traveled great distance to join us, the generous assistance of friends who helped with the event, the cards of congratulations from people whom we didn't even realize knew about it, and the honest and touching reactions of all the children we know were heartwarming and overwhelming. Although all our immediate family ended up attending and enjoying

Nora Skolnick and Laura Davidson of
Braintree, Vermont, in their greenhouse room

Nora is an elementary school teacher,
and Laura is an administrator at
Vermont Law School.

political smorgasbord. I found the legislative work both challenging and fascinating—a giant, complex problem to be solved. My motivation to complete the work came from a desire to prepare the best legislation possible, faithful to the law and the facts.

The workload was very intense and this, on top of the emotional and political content of the work, made for difficult times, particularly in terms of keeping my family and professional life intact. The process was hard on my family, who saw me less, and who often fielded difficult telephone calls or withstood stares and snickers. My wife, Susan, and our three children, were real troupers through the entire period.

What was special for me during the process? The way the Judiciary Committee came together to work as a team; we each learned a lot about ourselves and one another. We learned how hard we could work, and we learned about the discrimination and prejudice suffered by fellow committee members. What was also special were the many sincere and sometimes touching letters I received from all kinds of Vermonters, many in support, many opposed.

Representative Little learned an important lesson throughout the process and shares advice with others who may find themselves doing this kind of work. Do your homework and search for the most consistent reliable factual information before crafting a solution. The problem as initially perceived will not be the problem that you find, after diligent work, really needs to be solved. Fix the real problem, not the one that is initially or commonly perceived.

All in all, my recollections from the 2000 session are of a rich, complex and spicy stew of ideas, emotions, fears, legislative proposals, self-doubts, new working relationships, and of the eventual triumph of reason and compassion—and of the strength and patience of my family.

Tom Little seated at his desk in the House chamber

Tom served as a Republican member of the
Vermont House of Representatives from 1992 to 2002.
Tom is a lawyer in private practice and has been active in
many nonprofit organizations. He lives with his wife
Susan and their family in Shelburne, Vermont.

Joseph Watson and Michael Warner

Welcoming, warm, funny, genuine…time spent with Joseph and Michael brings these words to mind. For years, this couple has given their time and energy to civil rights reform for gay and lesbian Vermonters. Their dedication and talents peaked however, during the struggle for same-sex marriage.

Joseph remembers: Due to my work on adoption rights in the mid '90s, I was invited to help form the Vermont Freedom to Marry Task Force. By June of 1996, Michael and I became the first "poster couple" for the VFMTF, when a photo of us cutting the cake at our '93 commitment ceremony appeared on the front cover of the *Burlington Free Press.* That same year, I directed the production of the video *The Freedom to Marry: A Green Mountain View.*

By the late '90s, Michael and I were on the VFMTF board, doing general education and financial work. I attended the Supreme Court oral arguments and videotaped them for community access cable television. In 2000, we started working with the Action Committee and spent lots of time in Montpelier lobbying. We attended public hearings and committee meetings. The time we spent talking about this with others took over our lives.

The work we did resulted in the civil union law. We attended one of the first civil unions on July 1, 2000, and we celebrated our own civil union on July 7, 2000.

Joseph knew from the beginning that the journey would be difficult, but his faith in society's general progress toward enlightenment fed his determination to engage in this enduring challenge. His reactions to this work were varied and intense, but the two most powerful ones were pride and fear. I felt proud to be a Vermonter and proud of the history of the people of

Michael Warner and Joseph Watson live
"the quiet country life" in Leicester, Vermont.
They both work in the library at
Middlebury College.

Vermont. I was proud to be so close to some of the wonderful people who started the "freedom to marry" movement in Vermont and proud of their integrity and honesty. I was also proud of our public servants and representatives who dug deep and did the right thing.

At the same time I felt fear. I was afraid for the physical safety of beloved friends and other people in the struggle. I kept recalling others who had been murdered or injured just for speaking and living their beliefs. I was so relieved when we seemed to have arrived at the other side of the struggle with no severe casualties.

In a letter to the editor, Michael wrote: As a native Vermonter I am proud. I am proud of the seven generations that have come before me. I am proud of my Abenaki roots. I am proud of my Quaker relatives who stood firm against slavery. I am also proud of my Catholic and Québecois heritage. I am especially proud of my paternal grandmother who chose a path of quiet dignity, becoming a successful single mother in the 1930s—well before it was a socially acceptable thing to do. And, I am equally proud of my own parents, who, in the 1950s, chose to marry outside of the Catholic Church, in spite of intense pressure and coercion on my mother to convert. Each of my ancestors stood their ground for what they believed—knowing what was right for them, even in the face of strong opposition.

It is this level of pride and respect, which I have taken forward into my own civil union. I am extremely proud to be among the few Vermonters who have been able to benefit from the admirable good sense our Vermont legislators who passed the civil union law. In spite of our differences, we are all alike, wanting nothing more and nothing less than the same consideration, respect and dignity that my ancestors sought as they quietly went about their lives.

An event that reminds us of the tender and time-limited nature of life occurred on May 26, 2002. Michael's father, Bernie, died. Michael remembers, my father's death made me aware of how special the time was during the debate. He was diagnosed with cancer of the larynx in 1998, before much of the intensity of civil union began. Our family pulled together and brought him through that challenge as a changed man—physically, mentally, and spiritually. Joseph and I were there, along with my brother, to do whatever we could for both my parents. They had always respected Joseph and the wonderful human being that he is; however, this family crisis made them understand our love in more than an abstract way. It became real for them as their affection for him grew. My father referred to him as his third son.

All individuals deserve the right to live honestly, freely, and safely as the people they truly are. All families deserve the opportunity to know their loved ones in a true light. Marriage rights for gay and lesbian couples is one way a society can help validate what is important to the majority of people—family cohesion. In Michael's words, I am honored to have joined my life with someone whom I love and respect. Our individual families have become one. Our lives, individually, and our life together, deserve the same honor, respect and protections as those of each of our neighbors. ❧

Representative Steve Hingtgen

I grew up in Iowa. Catholic Iowa. I was an altar boy and an Eagle Scout. Although I'm not a spiritual person now, many of the lessons of the church stay with me as an adult, particularly "Love thy neighbor as thyself." I'm pretty sure my parents completely disagreed with my support for same-sex marriage and civil union, but they never offered their opinions and I never asked for them. Despite our possible difference of opinions, I thank them for instilling morality and for teaching me to love justice.

Little did I know how much this would help me in my work on the House Judiciary Committee during the civil union question. Making law is often more of an emotional process than people realize. Ultimately, I think the stark contrast between the advocates for and against same-sex marriage really struck me. No one could dismiss the quality of the testimony. The angry and ill-prepared opponents left a very bad taste in everyone's mouths.

Then there was the mail! Never could we have imagined how much mail and email we would receive. It was exciting but often disturbing. Hostile veiled threats. Tearful thanks. Damnation. Admiration. It arrived in piles in our mailboxes and on our computers. I've saved it all. I'm sure I'll look back on it many times in years to come. How else could I explain the experience to my grandchildren other than letting them page through the letters?

Through the pressure and schizophrenia of daily hostility on one side and deep appreciation on the other, our committee grew very close, even while recognizing there remained core differences in both our values and our political realities. We joked and laughed a lot. I remember joking with other committee members that "We're just trying to get gay and lesbian couples to stop living in sin." Considering how much we

Steve Hingtgen at the Scrumptious Café
in Burlington, Vermont

Steve was elected to a second term as
State Representative in November 2000.

disagreed with each other on every other issue that came before the committee, it still amazes me that we were unanimous on the importance of responding to the *Baker* decision in a way that respected gay and lesbian couples.

The majority of the committee clearly knew that marriage, and not a separate structure, would be the proper legal response to the *Baker* decision. It seemed to me that our committee had a responsibility to make that statement to the public and to other lawmakers. It was disappointing when we shied away from that position. On at least two occasions I told advocates I was having second thoughts about my support for civil union. I'm still not fully comfortable with it despite the broad praise.

And did the compromise of civil union help? I remember standing outside the polls on Election Day [2000] following the enactment of civil union. It was the third time I had stood before my neighbors to ask for their votes, but this election was different. It was the first time anyone had been openly hostile to me as they walked past me into the school to vote. Others were simply cold and didn't speak to me as they passed by.

Nevertheless, I'm so honored to have played a part in this process. It is my sincere hope that other states will quickly move to not just adopt civil union, but move past civil union to full marriage benefits for gay and lesbian couples. That will be the most exciting legacy of the *Baker* decision and the work of the Vermont legislature. ~

Christopher Tebbetts ~

We left the Statehouse in a snowstorm. The snow hadn't begun to fall when we arrived at five o'clock. Now, at eleven, my Subaru had a thick white coat, and it was coming down in big, flat flakes, the kind you can see the shape of in midair. We brushed off the car and headed toward the highway.

Four hours of testimony had been surprisingly un-boring. Something like fifteen hundred people had shown up, despite the coming snowstorm, either in support of or against same-gender marriage. By Vermont standards this was Quite A Big Deal, the heaviest turnout for a public hearing anyone could remember. Virtually everyone there wore some sort of sticker—either a bright pink one, "I Support the Freedom to Marry," or a white one, "Don't Mock Marriage."

The Judiciary Committee heard testimony from clergy, mothers, fathers, partners, husbands, wives, children. As each person approached the table in the center of the chamber, I made an exercise of looking at their faces before their chests. Would they be wearing a pink sticker or a white sticker? I guessed wrong about half of the time. If I looked down and saw a white sticker, I was disappointed as much as anything. It was like losing a friend, over and over.

Many of those testifying against us referred to "God's moral imperative." I heard that we were an abomination, that God did not create "Adam and Steve," that STDs run rampant among gay men, that we should love the sinner and hate the sin. I think I heard more Scripture than I've heard in one place, including church. I was numbed by the repetition.

Several days later, I would break down in tears suddenly, remembering what had been said, and re-experiencing it as a stinging injustice. While the hearing had been civil, it also felt archaic. Bigotry rose to the microphone that night, again and again, and was given an equal voice that racism or anti-Semitism or sexism would not be given today. In the days after, I had to force myself not to think about it too much.

During the hearing itself, however, my truth was a rock. I had no trouble hanging onto it. I left the Statehouse feeling tired but invigorated.

It was hard to use more than one lane on I-89. We crept along in a line of cars going about 35 miles an hour. The heater was just beginning to do its job, a few miles north of Montpelier, when I saw brake lights. I watched them in a chain reaction from car to car towards us, forcing me to slow down and eventually to stop. Someone was trying to push a van to the side of the road. One other car had pulled over to help, and we did the same.

The van had stalled on a bend in the highway. Despite the slow traffic, it was still a precarious place to be. I hadn't been able to see much more than a car length ahead of me just a few minutes ago, and the storm was getting worse.

There were four of us in our car—me, my boyfriend Jonathan, my sister Shelly and another friend, Erika. Between us, the other stranger who had stopped, and the driver of the van itself, we quickly got it pushed onto the shoulder. I hadn't really noticed but now saw three women inside the van. Wife, daughter and grandmother was an easy guess. Given the weather, it was also a good chance that anyone on this stretch of road was coming from the same place. The women sat very still, like deer, looking silently at the rest of us. I noticed at that moment that everyone who had stopped to help had bright pink stickers on their coats.

"I've got room for three," said the driver of the third car. His sticker proclaimed him as one of us.

"We'll wait here, you can go call for a tow," said the wife from inside the van.

"You can't wait here, you'll freeze to death," said the van driver. It sounded to me like something out of *Little House on the Prairie.*

There was no response. We all stood there shifting from foot to foot. Finally, the cold, wind and late hour pushed me to speak.

Michelle (Shelly) Teegarden of Essex, Vermont, works in college admissions. She and her husband Joe have two children. [Michelle's essay follows.]

Chris Tebbetts and Jonathan Radigan of Burlington, Vermont, are now joined in civil union. Chris is a writer and Jonathan is a health educator.

"Listen," I said, "this guy has three spaces, he can take three of you to where you're going. We have room for one more. Sir, we can take you to the next exit and you can call a tow truck from there."

Again, the van folks looked silently from one to the other. The rest of us, satisfied with the plan, scurried back to our cars.

When he finally joined us, the man from the van got in without a word. He squeezed next to Shelly and Erika in the back seat, and we took off.

Jonathan spoke first. "So, where are you coming from?" he asked. I could recognize a tinge of boldness behind the seemingly innocent question.

"Montpelier," said the man evenly.

My sister prodded a little more. "What were you..."

"We were at the hearing too," he said, with what I imagined was resignation.

"Oh."

More silence, and then Erika spoke up. "Do you have AAA?" she asked.

"Yeah," said the man, his voice less constricted than before, "in fact, I just joined last week. Good thing."

"That is a good thing," said my sister. "Chris, do you and Jonathan have AAA?"

"No," I said, my own mental gears turning.

"Oh you should get it."

"Yeah," I said, "but we can't get a family membership."

Again, no one said anything. The silence in the car felt somehow louder than the one before.

When we arrived at a Mobil station a few minutes later, the man thanked us, sincerely, for our help, got out of the car, and went inside. We crawled back onto the highway and continued north.

Michelle Teegarden ∾

"You know I'm gay, right?" These were the words that my brother Chris used to come out to our family almost 15 years ago. I was simultaneously relieved and flattered that I was the first member of our family to be told—the news was welcomed honesty. Over the next year or so, the remaining members of my family were informed and finally there were no more secrets. Chris eventually moved to Vermont from New York City, and we've grown closer ever since. I was fond of his partner, Jonathan, right away, and delighted in the wonderfully loving and synchronous relationship he shared with Chris. Jonathan quickly became an integral part of family gatherings, holidays and day-to-day life.

When the civil union debate heated up, Chris became a leader in the Freedom to Marry Task Force. I, too, became passionate about the passage of civil union, and began attending press conferences, Statehouse hearings, public forums and debates, and writing letters to the editor.

Throughout my life I have participated in support of a variety of liberal issues, but never have I felt more compelled to get involved and see something through than I did with civil union. It felt personal and urgent—it evoked strong emotion. It felt like our world simply could not be civilized unless gay and lesbian relationships were recognized with as much legitimacy and respect as heterosexual relationships. I felt righteous and certain that anyone in opposition to civil union was simply ignorant or afraid—no matter what their reasoning. Those "Take Back Vermont" signs, like a burning cross, triggered tremendous anger and fear in me.

For the first time in my life as a straight, white, upper-middle class woman, I experienced a sampling of the kind of harassment that gays and lesbians have been subjected to. It came in the form of anonymous phone calls, threatening body language and road rage. It was repulsive and disheartening. But it was the smallest price to pay. I was proud to be on the right side.

My children, then 11 and 15, experienced all this along with my husband and me. I'm delighted that they're old enough to be able to remember this historical event as they grow up. Their support of civil union is undaunted by the homophobia so common among their peers. On Election Day in November 2000, my son rode his bike over to the polling center near our home and questioned the people displaying anti-civil union posters. He asked them what it was about civil union that made them so afraid, and how could civil union ever hurt anyone? One man shoved a leaflet into Luke's hands with a promise that there were doctors that could give him some medicine to protect him from homosexual thoughts.

When the civil union law finally passed, I was elated and enormously proud of my brother's leadership and courage, proud of the legislators who supported its passage, and especially proud to be a resident of Vermont. Chris and Jonathan's civil union ceremony was performed in September 2000. The following July we gathered with 100 friends and family members at my home to celebrate their commitment to one another.

This experience defined friendships and relationships for me—strengthening some and establishing the end of others. I welcome these changes with no regrets and take joy in the positive impact that civil union will have on all of our lives. ❧

Senator Ann Cummings ~

In general I'm a compromise seeker, a peace-maker. I don't like to make decisions that cause pain for my constituents.

It was sometimes difficult for Vermont State Senator Ann Cummings to find herself in the middle of contentious debate during the fight for same-sex marriage. As the legislature immersed itself in the task of finding a remedy in response to the Supreme Court ruling, Ann and other legislators found themselves staring in the face of some very fundamental issues.

One controversial issue was that of religion. I'm Catholic. My pastor said what he thought, but he didn't attack me. So, unlike other legislators, I was able to keep going to church, and didn't receive any rejection from other parishioners. I didn't have to reconcile this issue with my religious beliefs. Being Catholic, and my relationship with my church, are my choice. There's a difference between state law and church law, and if I choose to follow a tenet of the church, it's my personal relationship with the church. I don't have a right to enforce my moral conscience, or my moral decisions, or my church's decisions, on anyone else.

It's hard for some people to understand that not everybody agrees with them, that all Christians don't agree on everything. Love really has no merit unless you can love your enemies. The same is true for freedom. There is no virtue in freedom if you can't allow freedom to people who do something you don't think they should.

Like most Americans, Ann believes in majority rule. But the civil union issue taught her the limitations of the concept. I wasn't surprised at the Supreme Court's decision, because it was based on our Constitution. The Constitution is the rule we agree to live by, a covenant that is meant to protect all of us; and the rule of law overrides popular opinion. There is a lack of understanding of this rule of law, this system of checks and balances. The legislature couldn't ignore the Supreme Court and the Court couldn't ignore the Constitution. This is one of the times when the people do not rule; it's done that way on purpose. The founding fathers believed in God, they were God-fearing people, but they were also men who believed in reason. The conflict between faith and reason was a primary conflict of their time; they were literally sitting down and drawing up a social compact to remedy the persecution they had felt in Europe. And they built a system so that nobody—not even "we the people"—could ever have absolute power. But during the civil union debate, it was very difficult for people to understand that they could be said "no" to, even if they were in the majority.

Some opponents of civil union let me know their opinions. Reading mail warning me of eternal damnation was tough. I got tons of that kind of mail every morning, lots from out-of-state. My husband's answering machine maxed out daily which made it difficult to do business. Our teenage children would answer our phone and get earfuls. Someone even published my office number. I work at an adult daycare facility, and my co-workers had to bear some of the brunt. It was also a risk to the agency to tie up the phone since we deal with elders. You know, my choice is my choice, but to place the burden on my family and co-workers is not right. Other people are not responsible for my vision or my choice. And even though all those affected were very supportive, that's what I felt was the worse part of it...the ramifications on other people.

Yet Senator Cummings managed to put things in perspective as she continued her legislative work. Toward the end of the session, as the Senate was trying to work out their version of the civil union bill, Ann recalls a now infamous St. Albans meeting. I went up to the meeting in order to support the work of Senator Kittell. The Senate Judiciary Committee was still taking testimony and we were still really tentative. As a person who seeks compromise, I was still trying to find a middle ground where most people could find some comfort. We went to St. Albans that night to give a rundown of the process, very technical things, not pro or con, just a rundown of the process. As we tried to address the gathering, we couldn't finish. The crowd just hooted and yelled. I think it's the first time I've ever been concerned about safety at a public meeting. There were no police present, and there were hundreds of angry, angry people. There was a 10-year-old boy wanting to say something good about his gay parents, and people were yelling despicable things at him. As I returned home that night I realized that there would be no compromise possible with these people, that nothing was going to make this easier, so...I'm not trying any more...that was it.

Ann Cummings, a state senator from Montpelier, Vermont, served on the Senate Judiciary Committee during the civil union debates.

have ordered that. I could not even imagine what was ahead, having to go through the legislature. Even with the *Baker* decision behind us, the very thought of that process was daunting and discouraging.

Friends not as immersed in this work could not understand my disappointment. Indeed, the ruling was an enormous positive step in gay rights. So, to the world I just put on the best possible face, in hopes that, in time, I myself would believe it was a win.

And in time—a lot of time—I did come to believe that. I now think the struggle that Vermont went through over this issue was the best possible public education tool that could have happened. By January 2000, there could not have been a Vermonter who hadn't heard of the same-sex marriage issue. The Court's decision put this issue in front of Vermonters, and provided a forum and context for public education, that we could never have achieved ourselves. I have wondered in retrospect whether, if the Court's ruling had been to open marriage to same-sex couples, there would have been impeachment hearings and a constitutional amendment process launched. The ruling facilitated the public education process to such a degree that, at this point, I have come to consider it a wise decision, even though it brought us an enormous battle.

"How did you become involved in the civil union process?" is a question I've been asked often—by press, students, volunteers, and the public—particularly if I let it slip that I am straight. If you're straight, people wonder why you are so involved in this gay rights issue. In a way, that question simply boggles my mind, because I fundamentally believe that if anyone is oppressed, we are all oppressed. To me this not just a cliché, or a nice rule to live by; I believe it is a fundamental truth. Oppression puts all of us in boxes. And I don't want a world where we're told how we should be, whether it's about our gender, race, religion, sexual orientation, wealth, intelligence, or anything else. I want a world where we appreciate our diversity, and recognize that our diversity is the very thing that makes "the whole being greater than the sum of the parts."

I've seen meanness toward people who are arbitrarily defined as somehow different, starting on the playground, and I've never understood it...the fat kid, the smart kid, the poor kid, the darker-skinned kid, the uncoordinated kid, the kid with braces or glasses, the kid whose mother isn't married. For me, this work was about same-sex marriage at one level. But at a more fundamental level, it was about oppression—all oppressions—versus the inherent worth and dignity of every person.

Through the work and struggle, a lot of really wonderful benefits came out of this experience for me. One is that I got to meet so many new and wonderful people. I

Dorothy Mammen of Middlebury, Vermont, served as statewide coordinator of the Vermont Freedom to Marry Task Force. She is the mother of two children.

was struck by how warmly volunteers and supporters embraced me. I was amazed, over and over again, by the level of integrity, caring, and articulateness that I experienced among the folks I worked with. I feel that I have made dozens, if not hundreds, of friends for life, all over Vermont.

Also, I got to know the state of Vermont a lot better than I had. I now know where almost every town is, and in many cases who the representatives and senators are, and who was supportive or negative on the issue. I spent a significant amount of time at the Statehouse and learned a tremendous amount about the legislative process. I learned to speak more forcefully for equal rights and social justice, including women's rights.

Were there any costs? I'm not sure. After I finished this work and was looking for other employment, I sometimes wondered whether the VFMTF line on my résumé might be taken as a negative in some places. Given some of the things I saw during the last two years, it wouldn't surprise me.

But I wouldn't change a thing. It's a part of who I am, and I'm never going back.

Senator Dick McCormack ~

I don't understand why gays and lesbians are so grateful to the legislature. We gave them the bare minimum the Constitution requires, nothing more. The Vermont Supreme Court interpreted the Vermont Constitution as guaranteeing the rights and responsibilities of civil marriage to gay and lesbian couples, and found that the existing marriage law violated the Constitution. Each legislator is bound by oath to uphold the Constitution. Therefore, we were bound to change the law to give gay and lesbian couples their constitutional rights. Simple.

Senator McCormack is known for his clearheaded and reasoned views. As a person who has been in favor of civil marriage for gay and lesbian couples and against any "separate but equal" solution, he had no doubts on where he stood in the gay marriage debate. Using basic principles such as constitutional primacy, judicial review, separation of church and state, and the primacy of individual constitutional rights over the tyranny of the majority, he built his arguments on a strong logical foundation.

However, there was more to the story than logic. On the Senate floor, I said that if something is worth thinking clearly about, it's worth feeling deeply about. To lead only with the heart is sentimentality. To lead only with the intellect is to risk becoming a monster. Thomas Jefferson wrote of an ongoing conversation between his heart and mind. So this was with me.

Underlying my logic was empathy for gay and lesbian people. Life is hard for the luckiest of us, under the best of circumstances. I'm bothered by the thought that nice people are hurt and insulted because of a part of them as vulnerable and tender as their sexuality. It's pointlessly unkind, and it makes me sad, and it makes me angry.

Dick McCormack's resolve to fight for gay marriage rights was fueled by his disdain for the tactics and attitudes of the opposition. He found their arguments weak and filled with a moralizing, scolding, self-pitying tone. One of the worst displays he recalled was at a civil union hearing in St. Albans. The opposition was out in force to demonstrate the intensity of their feelings. Well, they did. It was ugly, stupid, hateful, and frustrating. They berated a little boy. They roared in deep tones and hysterical screaming. A journalist sitting next to me asked with torment in his eyes, "Is it always this ugly?" *The only benefit to that meeting was that the behavior pushed key people to their final decision to support civil union.*

As the debates wound down and the time to vote drew near, it became clear that civil union, rather than gay marriage, would be the strategy. Public opinion was strong and the votes for marriage weren't there. I'll never forget the sadness on Representative Bill Lippert's face when he and Representative Tom Little and I discussed the need to back away from marriage. *Believing that individual constitutional rights trump public opinion in any case, Dick McCormack was deeply troubled by this decision.* But, I agreed to defer to public opinion and support only what the Constitution required.

Like many Vermonters, Senator McCormack understands the positive aspects of creating civil union while at the same time regretting the failure to obtain full marriage rights for gay and lesbian couples. The arguments were clear, the logic was clear, the emotional instincts were admirable and right. We had the legal backing to create gay marriage, but the political support was not there. Even so, my part in this effort is one of the best things I ever did as a legislator. We did a good thing.

Richard J. (Dick) McCormack of Bethel, Vermont,
at his desk in the Senate chamber

He served as Democratic State Senator from Windsor County,
Senate Majority Leader and Vice Chair of the Judiciary Committee
during the civil union issue. Dick is a former history teacher,
father of two sons, and has two granddaughters.

Greg Trulson and Willie Docto ~

We met in the fall of 1992 at a gay-owned log home bed and breakfast in the mountains of West Virginia. Little did we know that four years later, we would buy our very own log home and turn it into a B&B in the Green Mountains of Vermont. The Moose Meadow Lodge officially opened in 1998. From the start, it has attracted a gay and lesbian as well as straight clientele.

During the *Baker* lawsuit, before the case even reached the Vermont Supreme Court, we were skeptical. How could the state ever grant the plaintiffs marriage licenses? We thought it was a nice try, but that not much would come of it. Of course, we were both pleasantly surprised by the decision.

We listened to the testimony on the radio. We attended the debates at the Statehouse. We couldn't understand the fears expressed by the opponents of the civil union bill. However, we were very surprised by the support of non-gay people who spoke passionately and intelligently on behalf of the bill.

We participated in the Millennium March on Washington in April 2000, just days after the civil union law was signed by Governor Dean. We marched with the Vermont contingent. It was heartening to see and hear the spectators cheer and roar when the Vermont group passed them by. Many spectators were in tears.

What has the civil union law done for us personally?

We both come from very religious families: one family of strict Roman Catholics who pray the rosary each night, and the other a family of strict Bible-based Protestants. However, both of our families have accepted us and our relationship with open arms. We believe that having had our own civil union has helped our relatives feel more

Willie Docto and Greg Trulson at
Moose Meadow Lodge in Duxbury, Vermont

Willie is an association management consultant, violinist, and innkeeper. Greg is an I/T architect specialist, justice of the peace, and innkeeper.

comfortable about treating us as a couple. First, it demonstrated our lifetime commitment to each other. Secondly, it gives everyone no doubt that we are a couple. They treat us as a family unit. Our relatives ask about both of us on the phone or through emails. Our nieces and nephews consider both of us as their uncles. We're both expected to attend holidays, weddings, or other family gatherings. Invitations are addressed to "Greg and Willie."

Most, if not all, of our associates appreciate the significance and importance of the right to have a civil union. Willie serves on the board of a statewide nonprofit organization. The day before our civil union, at a board meeting of this group, Willie informed key people that he would have to leave early to make last-minute preparations for our civil union. The chair, several staff and board members were genuinely excited to hear about the civil union, and warmly extended their congratulations.

We were also pleased by how supportive our neighbors in Duxbury have been. Duxbury is a small town of about 1,200 people, but wonderfully progressive and accepting. When we had our civil union, we limited our guest list to around 30. This meant that many of our friends, neighbors, associates, and even family were not invited. One day, about six months after our ceremony, Willie bumped into our next-door neighbor at the grocery store. The neighbor came up to Willie and said with a slight grin, "I'm mad at you!" Knowing it was a friendly tease, Willie asked, "Oh really? Why's that?" The neighbor replied, "Because I wasn't invited to your civil union."

In relation to our business, civil unions are very good for Vermont's economy. Since the civil union law was passed, our gay and lesbian clientele has increased from 20 to 60 percent. In the 20 months following the law's passage, the Moose Meadow Lodge hosted nearly 60 civil union ceremonies. The civil union law also inspired Greg to run for justice of the peace, and he has officiated at more than 50 civil unions.

When all is said and done, it's not hard to find many fine reasons for the continued support of this important step toward inclusion and equality.

Susan Murray and Karen Hibbard ~

The attainment of civil rights has historically required the ongoing commitment of dedicated leaders. For each of the individuals who were visibly engaged in the fight for same-sex marriage, there were partners and family members who gave as generously through their enduring support behind the scenes. Karen Hibbard and Susan Murray reflect on their partnership in this effort.

Karen

For as long as Susan and I have been together—16 years now—she has worked on cases involving gay and lesbian rights. I've watched her work to change the laws for the better and I've been so proud of her. I've felt like I was watching history being made.

When Susan began working on the same-sex marriage case, I knew that she would be very busy, and that our relationship and our lives would be disrupted in many ways. But this felt bigger than me, and bigger than us, and I knew this issue needed Susan's full attention and expertise in order for it to succeed. And I knew it would succeed, because with people like Susan and Beth Robinson and Mary Bonauto working on it, there was no way we were going to lose!

There were times in this process when I felt very scared, especially for Susan's physical safety; there were a lot of angry people out there who seemed to feel entitled to condemn us and our lives. But my overall feeling is one of pride, for all those people, gay and straight, who came out publicly and worked to support our fight for our civil rights.

When the Supreme Court decided *Baker,* I felt as though we had been given a great gift. And when the legislature finally passed the civil union law, I felt validated—as though a part of my life, which had gone unrecognized for so long, was finally being recognized as important and valid and worthy of respect.

Susan

Where do I begin? It has been more than two years since civil union became law, and time has softened the edges for me. With some exceptions, my life is more or less back to its normal pace, but without a doubt, my experiences during the last seven years have been life-changing. I have literally hundreds of memories—some joyful, some exquisitely painful, but all of them poignant.

I have fond memories of marathon conferences with my friends and colleagues, Beth Robinson and Mary Bonauto, as we debated, negotiated, and fine-tuned our legal arguments in the *Baker* case. They are two of the most intelligent lawyers and outstanding human beings I will ever have the privilege to know.

I vividly remember our preparations for the oral argument before the Vermont Supreme Court. For several weeks we had been trying, unsuccessfully, to distill the essence of this complicated legal issue into the half-hour presentation the Court had allotted to us. Then one night, it all came together. I remember sitting on the floor in Beth's living room, leaning against her couch as she stood a few feet away. She began to talk about a case [*Perez v. Lippold*] that had played a central role in our briefs: a 50-year-old interracial marriage case from California. In the face of overwhelming popular opposition, the justices in that case had struck down California's ban on interracial marriages. Why not simply urge the Vermont Supreme Court to lead this country in the same way, by doing what was courageous, and correct, in this case? When she'd finished speaking, I pounded my fist in exultation; I knew it was the straightforward, eloquent presentation we'd been searching for.

The day of the oral argument is indelibly etched in my mind. Hordes of local and national reporters and television camera crews crowded the hallways of the courthouse. Spectators started arriving before dawn, standing outside in the frigid November morning, hoping to claim a seat in the tiny courtroom; security guards were forced to issue tickets and set up overflow seating in the hallways. It was so crowded that we couldn't squeeze through the courtroom door to reach counsel table; instead, we had to be ushered into the courtroom the back way, through the justices' chambers. The arguments, and the justices' questions, were riveting. The air was electric with expectation and excitement. There was a palpable sense that history was being made.

Karen Hibbard and Susan Murray

Karen is a physician assistant. Susan, an attorney at Langrock Sperry & Wool, served as co-counsel to the plaintiffs in *Baker v. State of Vermont.*

December 20, 1999—the day the Court issued its decision in *Baker*—was an exhausting, emotionally complicated day for me. We had been prepared to win, and we had been prepared to lose. We were not prepared for what we got: a "win" without a remedy. I remember reading the Court's long opinion in the car as Beth drove us to the press conference we'd scheduled, feeling a confusing mixture of joy and despondency, and I remember thinking with dread about the fate to which the Court had just consigned us: difficult, politically-charged debates in the legislature.

And then, at the end of that long day, something wonderful happened. An impromptu meeting had been scheduled at the Unitarian church in Burlington, so people interested in the case could gather to talk about the decision. Beth and I had been asked to speak, to explain the Court's ruling. When we entered the building, I saw to my astonishment that there were hundreds of people in the pews. When we stepped to the microphone, they stood and cheered, a long and raucous and jubilant applause, and I was completely taken aback. That moment confirmed for me that this struggle was about much more than the bundle of legal benefits that comes with a marriage license. It was fundamentally about legal and societal recognition and respect for gay and lesbian families. That night helped give me the strength I needed to make it through the ensuing political battles.

From January through mid-April of 2000, Beth and I put our law practices on hold. We spent many long and exhausting days at the legislature, testifying, cajoling, devising strategies, drafting proposed language, compromising, listening, waiting, hoping.

Some of those days stand out, such as the first day of hearings, when I testified in a tiny committee room crowded with spectators and camera crews; and the day the House Judiciary Committee voted, in an extraordinarily emotional session, to create the institution of "civil union" rather than open the marriage laws to gay and lesbian couples. Then there were the two tense days of debate on the House floor, when the outcome of the bill was in doubt until the very end; and the two days of debate in the Senate, when some lawmakers spoke so eloquently they left many in the crowd in tears.

I remember with immense pride and gratitude the hundreds of supporters, gay and straight, young and old, parents and religious leaders, who flocked to the Statehouse to talk with their legislators and drove through blizzards to testify at packed public hearings. I remember the overwhelming piles of mail the legislators got on this issue, and the thousands of letters to the editor. I remember conversations with individual lawmakers in the coatroom and hallways and cafeteria, and the quiet moments of humor and kindness we shared. I remember the thoughtfulness and courage with which many lawmakers supported civil union, in the face of immense public pressure.

And I will never forget the moments immediately following the final vote on the bill. News media from around the world swarmed the floor of the House, trying to interview the three gracious couples we had represented in *Baker.* Crowds of lawmakers and citizens were laughing and hugging and taking pictures. I stood apart, watching the scene unfold as though in slow motion, and suddenly realized I was crying. We hadn't achieved full equality, but we'd won a remarkable victory nonetheless.

The ensuing campaign season was a depressing denouement. I was embarrassed and discouraged by the vitriol of some of my fellow Vermonters, and contemptuous of those politicians who encouraged the rancor for their own political advantage.

As I look back, I am keenly aware that few lawyers are lucky enough, in their professional lifetimes, to work on cases involving issues of important public policy. Even fewer of us have the privilege to work on a case involving groundbreaking issues of constitutional law and civil rights. And very, very few are able to combine that legal work with grassroots organizing, lobbying, political campaigning and fundraising, media experiences and speech-making. No matter how many years I practice law, and no matter how many successes I may have, *Baker v. State of Vermont* will always stand as the highlight of my legal career.

I have no doubt that, fifty years from now, gay and lesbian couples will be able to marry in every state in this country, and people will look back and wonder what the hullabaloo was all about in 2000. I'll be forever grateful that, thanks to the unwavering support of my law firm and especially Karen, my wonderful partner-in-life, I was able to play a part in this historic struggle.

Governor Howard Dean ~

How will the passage of civil union impact the children of Vermont? Governor Dean, also a medical doctor, has been a steady, impassioned supporter of issues affecting children throughout his tenure. Citing the difficult road for gay and lesbian youth, including an increased tendency toward suicide, Dean believes that the civil union law is a step in the right direction. "Giving these young Vermonters hope for the future and validity for who they are is important," *he says.*

His views include children who live in families with lesbian or gay parents. Vermont's adoption laws have always taken the best interest of the child into consideration first, the courts are clear on that. Civil unions can only add to the strength of families. *Prior to civil union, it was ironic that a child from a gay or lesbian home could have a legal relationship with each parent, yet the parents could not have a legal relationship with one another. Civil union provides a limited remedy to that problem.*

Governor Dean's support for civil union came naturally and quickly. As soon as the Supreme Court handed down their ruling, I knew where I stood. This is the right thing to do. I believe in the innate dignity and humanity of all people; therefore, I believe all people ought to be treated respectfully. This is an equal rights issue.

I recall the first time someone came out to me...I was in med school. He was a friend of mine and I cared about him, so I wanted to get to know more about him. What I often discover is that people have more in common as human beings and have a small number of differences.

Dean admits that he had to move through his own discomfort to see gay and lesbian people in a truer light. He believes that those who are opposed to lesbian and gay equal rights in general,

Governor Howard Dean, M.D.
in the Ceremonial Office at the
Statehouse in Montpelier, Vermont

and to civil union in particular, are in two categories. The first are those whose oppositions are based on their personal problems with the issue. The second are those who are uncomfortable due to their limited understanding of gays and lesbians. There is a lot of folklore surrounding homosexuals. People need to make an effort to learn the truth of the matter.

Such folklore was used to justify reasons why lesbian and gay couples should not be granted equal protection under the law. One popular concern was that Vermont would be swamped with new gay and lesbian citizens, that Vermont would become "Provincetown North." Governor Dean smiled at this notion. I believe that if more gay and lesbian people move to Vermont, our state will be strengthened by the addition of people who value family life and will be very good citizens. Vermont ought to do everything it can to support all of its citizens.

As a man of faith, Dean maintains the boundary between the religious and legal aspects of marriage. These ought to be separate and worked through accordingly. *As a man of science, he believes that society will continue to learn more about sexual orientation and its biological underpinnings. He questions how people can be treated so badly because of a biologically determined quality.*

As for the future, Governor Dean believes that people will continue to do a better job at this and that progress will continue even with its peaks and valleys. ❧

Annette L. Cappy ~

During the first four months of 2000, the legislative work that led to the creation of the civil union law was in full swing. Brattleboro's Town Clerk, Annette Cappy, remembers: I had not given this new law a great deal of thought except in terms of my role in administering it. I had been in favor of the legislation and a supporter, but had not been involved. I hadn't really given much thought to how it might affect me personally. *However, at the very moment June 30, 2000 gave way to July 1, 2000, Annette Cappy's personal experience with civil union began.*

When the civil union law went into effect on July 1, I willingly opened my office at midnight for a Brattleboro couple who wanted their ceremony as soon as the law permitted. As it turned out, the license I issued was the first civil union license issued in Vermont, and the ceremony held immediately following was the first civil union ceremony to take place in Vermont.

Her reason for opening the Town Clerk's office at midnight had to do with the timing of July 1 in the year 2000. I felt it was unfortunate that this new law, one that would be so important for so many people, was about to take effect for the first time, not only on a Saturday when most clerks' offices would be closed, but also on a long Fourth of July holiday weekend. Opening my office at that hour was not an attempt to make a statement, but in doing so, I realize I did make one, one that I am now very proud of. At the time it just felt like the right thing to do for a couple who had waited so long for something that was so important to them.

As that first Saturday continued, Annette recalls a powerful moment. One of the licenses I issued was to a couple who had been together several years. One of the gentlemen was in his seventies. When we finished with the legal paperwork, he reached out across the counter for my hand and said with tears in his eyes, "You'll just never know what this means." His words and tears touched me with such force. We just stood there holding onto each other's hand, and then hugged, both of us crying. Even now, when I think back on that moment, I have to fight back tears. I believe that was the beginning of my understanding of just what civil union is all about. That's when I got it. Our connection that morning made a lasting impression on me.

Now, two years after the inception of civil union, Annette realizes how deeply so many impressions have touched her. I have met couples that have come from nearly every state in the nation and some from foreign countries. It still surprises and saddens me when I see in their eyes the hesitation, and sometimes even fear, that some couples show when they come into the office. Most have absolutely no idea what kind of reception they will encounter when they approach my desk and tell me why they have come, and that says so much. The courage and strength it takes to come to a place that will allow them to publicly be themselves fills me with awe. These couples have no idea how they have enriched my life.

I know that opponents have argued that civil unions are demeaning to the sanctity of marriage. I don't understand that. In fact, what I feel is quite the contrary. Most couples I have come to know have been long-term, deeply committed couples who are only now beginning to enjoy the rights and privileges that the majority of Vermonters have always taken for granted. Since that first July weekend, I have come to appreciate and treasure my own husband and family even more, for now I realize that not everyone has had the privilege to be able to form a public, legal union with the person they intend to spend the rest of their life with.

Annette Cappy at the Brattleboro Town Clerk's Office. Annette was born and raised in Brattleboro, Vermont and has served as town clerk for 13 years. She has four children and six grandchildren.

Ethel Brosnahan ~
with Vivienne Armstrong and Louise Young

The creation of civil union in Vermont has not only brought loving couples together in legally recognized union, it has been a catalyst for amazing new friendships. People who may have never crossed paths have been brought together by this historic event. When Ethel Brosnahan, a justice of the peace in Brattleboro, agreed to be a participant in this project, she decided to include her two new friends in her photo. Vivienne Armstrong and Louise Young are a couple from Texas who came to Vermont to experience a right they have worked for their entire adult lives.

Ethel Brosnahan

My involvement in the civil union movement was a natural progression because of my position as a justice of the peace. When civil union became legal on July 1, 2000, I was automatically in the arena of one of the most historic events in Vermont.

The process of uniting same-sex couples was not much different for me than uniting heterosexual couples, except for one major factor. I was performing ceremonies for couples, like Vivienne and Louise, who had waited an extremely long time in their relationships to be united as a couple. I learned that whether a person is straight or gay doesn't matter. Their love and respect for each other is evident. The feelings I witness while performing these ceremonies are those of love, sincerity, and overall commitment to each other. Often there are children involved, and it is evident that the people who are present at these ceremonies for the couples love them deeply.

I have performed more than 200 civil union ceremonies and the proud feeling I get while officiating at these ceremonies is as strong as ever. There have been instances when I have been criticized by family and friends for participating in these ceremonies. However, I try not to get into a power struggle with anyone, since I am doing this for my own reasons and satisfaction. I have never been someone who discriminates against

Ethel Brosnahan (standing) with
Louise Young and Vivienne Armstrong

Ethel has worked in the Vermont Court system for 31 years. Among the positions she has held are court officer, sheriff's department officer, assistant judge, and justice of the peace. Louise, a software engineer, and Vivienne, a home health care nurse, are long-time lesbian civil rights activists.

people because of their ethnic, religious, or sexual persuasion. But no matter what I say to some people, it wouldn't make any difference.

I would like to share an extremely special and meaningful moment that stands out. Two gentlemen came up north from Florida to celebrate their 43rd anniversary together and wanted to be united as a couple on that date. They waited 43 years for this monumental occasion. During their ceremony, after they placed rings on each others' fingers, they took off those rings and brought out and slipped on the original rings they gave to each other 43 years ago. Neither one of them had felt that they would live long enough to witness a civil union taking place for them. That says it all.

I am truly honored to be an integral part of this historical event. In my own small way, I feel that I have made a significant difference in the lives of these people. Yet, I am the one who has gained from this experience and am a better person because of it.

Vivienne Armstrong and Louise Young

In the spring of 1971 when we met, fell in love and decided to spend the rest of our lives together, we said that we would only have a ceremony when we could legally do so. We also made a commitment to personally work to make this possible. For 29 years we worked and waited. Then Vermont passed the landmark civil union legislation.

We chose Brattleboro for the site of our July 2000 civil union because of the widespread publicity of the first civil union. We were so moved by the courage of Brattleboro Town Clerk, Annette Cappy, to open her office at midnight on July 1 to allow a couple to have their civil union as soon as possible that we wanted to go to her town.

On the day of our civil union, we arrived early at the Municipal Center. We were nervous about the license application process at the Town Clerk's Office, but Mrs. Cappy and her staff were warm and friendly and the form was simple and brief. Our Justice of the Peace, Mrs. Ethel Brosnahan, a kind and wonderful woman, put us at ease by going over the ceremony's words with us. She proudly pointed out that we would say "spouse" as part of our vows.

Soon we were on the Brattleboro Common's bandstand steps. Tears welled in our eyes and our voices quavered as we exchanged words that expressed the lifetime of love and commitment we had already shared. We slipped on matching rings. Then Mrs. Brosnahan said the words that we had waited a lifetime to hear: "By the power vested in me by the State of Vermont..." We were staggered by the enormity of it all.

Little did we know that having our civil union would change the course of our lives. After our civil union, we kept in touch with both Mrs. Cappy and Mrs. Brosnahan. We worked for the re-election of Governor Howard Dean and traveled to Montpelier for his inauguration in January 2001.

Although the courts have yet to decide whether a Vermont civil union is legal in other states, we felt the only way to ensure we could enjoy the full benefit was to move to Vermont. Therefore, we moved from Dallas, Texas to Brattleboro, Vermont in September 2001. Our home in Brattleboro is only nine miles north of the Massachusetts border and three miles west of the New Hampshire border. But to us that small distance makes all the difference in the world. If we lived more than nine miles south, we could not make medical decisions for each other without costly legal documents. If we lived more than three miles east, we could not have inheritance rights without costly legal documents. And these are only two of the many new legal rights we now have as residents of Vermont with a civil union.

We pulled up 25 years of Texas roots and moved to Vermont because we wanted our legal rights so much. Was it worth it? All we know is that we couldn't live the rest of our lives without the experience.

Roddy and Bill Cleary ~

It was 1969, the year Sister Roderick, a Roman Catholic nun, and Father William Cleary, a Jesuit priest, met. Being fully involved in the world events during a time of tremendous change and upheaval, these two passionate and deeply spiritual people also began a transformation in their personal lives. After much soul-searching, they decided to leave their respective vocations, marry, and become Roddy and Bill Cleary. They had two sons, Tom and Neil, and moved to Burlington, Vermont, in 1976. In the early days, they ran an interfaith bookstore. Roddy now teaches Women's Spirituality at the University of Vermont and serves as an Affiliate Minister at the First Unitarian Universalist Society Church in Burlington. Bill devotes himself to his writing and his music.

Roddy and Bill have made an indelible impression on the lives of many people. It is no surprise that their involvement in the same-sex marriage endeavor has been constant and true.

Roddy

For me, this time in Vermont history is part of an ongoing revelation. If God is love, then this affirmation of the beauty and goodness of gay and lesbian relationships gives added dimension and meaning to this revelation. I believe that civil unions are destined to strengthen the fabric of society.

Working with couples in preparation for their ceremonies has been an added bonus in my own life. I have been personally enriched. I have been privileged. It has given me new cause to wonder and give thanks for the grace of relationship and the extravagant nature of love.

A friend of mine asked me after the civil union of her friend, "Roddy, have you ever been in the presence of such joy?" Her question captured my own experience of

Bill Cleary and Roddy O'Neil Cleary
at their home in Burlington, Vermont

Sandi and Bobbi Côté-Whitacre ~

We almost decided not to have a civil union. *This declaration may seem surprising coming from a couple who worked diligently in the fight for same-sex marriage. But, Sandi and Bobbi were working for* marriage, *not some reasonable facsimile, such as civil union.*

The Baker v. State of Vermont *lawsuit was undertaken to win marriage rights for lesbian and gay couples. The Vermont Supreme Court upheld the legal basis for that right. However, rather than granting same-sex couples the right to marry, the Court handed the job of "crafting" the details of this right to the Vermont Legislature. The result of that work, civil union, was considered a compromise. Sandi and Bobbi believe that* the only ones who compromised were the people who were denied their full rights. The opponents of same-sex marriage didn't compromise; they were against same-sex marriage, they are against civil union, and they would take it away if given the chance.

Even though Bobbi and Sandi understood the desire of the legislature to find relative comfort for everyone, they also knew that the price for that comfort would fall on the shoulders of the people who continued to be marginalized. There comes a time in every civil rights movement when the carrot is dangled in front of the fighters, when the words "wait" and "don't go so fast" are heard in the court of public opinion. The carrot of compromise was dangling in front of us, and after much soul-searching, we came to the conclusion that to reach for this carrot would hurt not only those of us fighting for our rights now; it would condemn future generations to decades of work dismantling this compromise.

History often reminds us of this dilemma. One example in 1896 was the case of Plessy v. Ferguson, *in which the U.S. Supreme Court upheld lower court rulings that supported the "separate but equal" racial laws. The lone dissenter was Justice John Harlan.* Harlan said, "The destinies of the two races in this country are indissolubly linked together, and the

Sandi and Bobbi Côté-Whitacre, with
Bobbi's mother, Betty Whitacre

Sandi and Bobbi worked with the Vermont Freedom
to Marry Task Force from 1996 through 2001.
They live in Colchester, Vermont.

interests of both require that the common government of all shall not permit the seeds of hatred to be planted under the sanction of law." Now replace "races" with "orientations."

Sandi and Bobbi see a parallel with civil union. What can more certainly arouse hate, what can more certainly create and perpetuate a feeling of distrust between gays and straights, than state enactments which in fact proceed on the ground that gays and lesbians are so inferior and degraded that they cannot be allowed to marry like straights? That is the real meaning of such legislation as civil union, the thin disguise of "equal" benefits for couples in committed relationships. We, as a movement, must continue to stay the course; we must stay focused on the "rights" of marriage and not just the "benefits." Civil rights can never be decided by a plebiscite, and we cannot agree to give up our human rights without admitting we are less than human. We don't have the right to take the immediate partial benefits that are being dangled in front of us at the expense of future generations.

Nevertheless, on July 1, 2000, the civil union bill became law. The paradoxical nature of this law leaves many Vermonters feeling elated and validated by having their relationships legally recognized, while still feeling like second-class citizens. Bobbi and Sandi hope that this compromise will encourage those who don't feel comfortable with same-sex marriage to take the opportunity to see lesbian and gay relationships in a positive light.

When asked why they decided to be joined in civil union, Sandi and Bobbi smiled and looked at Betty Whitacre, Bobbi's 85-year-old mother, who said, "I just wanted the opportunity to see them get married. I didn't want to run out of time."

To ensure this opportunity, Betty's support went beyond the personal. Using her message, "They can't do this to my girls," *the Vermont Freedom to Marry Task Force sent out a fundraising letter that brought in thousands of dollars.*

Betty understands the concerns of Bobbi and Sandi, because as a very religious person she wanted them to marry in a church. And even though their civil union was not full-fledged marriage, she was proud to say that there were three ministers at Bobbi and Sandi's ceremony. She is grateful to have witnessed her daughter and daughter-in-law's wedding—so much so, that she celebrated by dancing with "her girls" at their reception!

Jim and Betsy Moore ~

The institution of marriage is at the core of this society's value structure. Most people are taught to look forward to this inevitable life event, and many do so with anticipation and excitement. Betsy Moore is no exception. Most parents pass along this expectation of marriage and often build up their hopes for the future. However, some children grow to follow an unexpected path. Jim and I are very committed to marriage. We have been together forever—35 years—and we raised our two children with that value. When our son, Brian, came out to us as a gay man, this was the one dream we thought we would have to relinquish.

Letting go of dreams can involve pain. The picture has changed and grieving the loss of those hopes can be very difficult for some parents. With time and support many people learn to adjust. When we speak to new parents in PFLAG, we always talk to them about giving up their own dreams for their child and taking on new ones.

Making room for dreams based on reality can create amazing joy. Vermont's quest for same-sex marriage resulted in new hope for many families. In our case, Brian gave us back our dream. We wanted a solid, lifelong love for him and along came Tom Robinson with the same family ideals. Civil union allowed them to realize their dreams of marriage and commitment.

Brian and Tom's union took place in two stages. They surprised us by arranging their legal union on July 15, which is our wedding anniversary. We were so honored that they chose this date and now we will share our anniversaries forever. The ceremony was a private one with a justice of the peace and the dear friend who introduced them. We celebrated at dinner and looked forward to the spiritual union to be held in October.

Why a second ceremony? We all believe that such an important commitment should really be made in the presence of family and friends, those who love you and will support you, then and in the future. This was how the spiritual union was planned. *Betsy remembers the moment,* I walked down the chapel aisle that day, I looked over at Tom's mom walking down the other aisle and at all the smiling faces in between. I knew that Brian and Tom had a loving and supportive community, just as Jim and I had thirty-five years ago. This is the gift of civil union to our family.

We live in Florida, and all our friends there told us not to get our hopes up for this law, but somehow we just knew it was going to pass. We keep Vermont and all those who worked so hard for its passage close to our hearts. They helped give us back our dream for our son and our new son-in-law. ❧

Betsy and Jim Moore with their son Brian
at Burlington, Vermont's 2002 Gay Pride March

Betsy and Jim, formerly from Massachusetts,
now live in Estero, Florida.

Mike Backman and Steve Swayne

Whether the civil union law was a compromise or a sell-out is a matter of opinion. Compromise is a term of negotiation indicating the settlement of a dispute by mutual concession. While it seems that some people in favor of same-sex marriage entered the compromise of civil union in good faith, and by doing so accepted the "separate but equal" scenario, those in opposition to same-sex marriage did not. The "compromise" was not honored. Within a year after civil union became law, gay and lesbian Vermonters, along with their allies, were back at the Statehouse testifying in front of a newly appointed House Judiciary Committee who wanted to repeal, or at least water down, civil union. In May 2001, Mike Backman and Steve Swayne from Woodstock once again opened their private thoughts and feelings to a group of politicians in hopes of encouraging them to finally see our common humanity.

Many of you on this committee want to take away our recognition of family. You try to define family the way it works for you, and try to impose that definition on all the rest of us in the state. When I was a child, I was taught by my parents and the society around me that there were other restrictions that should also define a family. I was taught that two people of different races should not ever consider falling in love and marrying. The rules of my church at the time, and the laws of many states, prevented a white and black person from being recognized and celebrated as a family. I remember well when society began to change and be more open to interracial relationships. There were many who tried to stop that trend—good, upstanding Christian people who were concerned with the moral decay of society. Most of us today have moved well beyond their attitudes, and we often shake our heads at their efforts to try and keep the traditions of racial purity alive.

Like them, some of you are now trying to turn back this recent societal change—the acceptance and celebration of gay and lesbian couples. You sit in your conservative

Steve Swayne and Mike Backman of Woodstock, Vermont

Steve is from Pasadena, California, and Mike is from Provo, Utah. They met while attending the Metropolitan Community Church of San Francisco in 1991. In 1999 they moved to Vermont when Steve began a job as a music professor at Dartmouth College.

circles and focus on the excesses of the gay community. This is like judging your marriages, your relationships, and your lives by comparing them to a spring break fraternity party in Florida. To judge all straight people on the excesses and extremes of the heterosexual lifestyle is wrong—and it is wrong for you to judge my family and my relationship on negative stereotypes you may harbor as well. It is nothing short of hypocrisy for those of you who criticize the promiscuity and excesses of the gay world and then attempt to pull out from under us the very institution that seeks to combat the excesses you so abhor. Civil union is a conservative measure, one that encourages young gays and lesbians to settle down and commit themselves to one relationship.

The public ceremonial aspect of civil union—registering with your town clerk and having a ceremony in front of a clergy person or a justice of the peace is a crucial element of the law. Our commitments to one another should be celebrated, need to be celebrated. There are few couples—gay or straight—who can survive alone, without the support of family and friends and of the community around them. Public ceremonies, both marriages and civil unions, are what bring a community together to honor and pledge support to any couple.

At our civil union, we had approximately 160 people at our home. About twenty of our guests were gay. That means 140 straight people witnessed our civil union. These couples, these parents, these children, these straight people, welcomed us into their lives. They celebrated with us the triumph of love over all the odds. They were genuinely happy for us. Our civil union strengthened their love for one another. It did not threaten or diminish or weaken their love or their marriages or their beliefs. Taking the public, ceremonial aspect out of our relationships tears at the very heart and soul of the civil union measure, and equates our relationships to a person obtaining a hunting license or registering a dog. This goes against the entire spirit of the *Baker* decision.

No one is asking each of you to personally accept gay couples and civil union, just as no one is asking you to personally accept interracial relationships. Those of you who oppose homosexuality or interracial marriages should teach your children in your homes and Sunday schools what you feel to be right or wrong. But these personal, mostly religious views do not belong in the laws of Vermont. Our state prides itself on its long history of treating everyone with dignity and respect. Civil union extends this equality to my family.

In closing, it is unconscionable that many of you are ready to repeal the civil union law without ever having attended a civil union. Come to our ceremonies, come into our homes and spend a day with us. See how we live, and how civil union is changing our lives and the lives of those around us for the better. You, as leaders, have an ethical requirement to walk a mile in our shoes before making a decision that so affects our lives. Please, our lives are open, our homes are open, our ceremonies are open. We invite you in.

Mary Hurlie

I am not sure if it was intense anger or deep, deep sadness...probably both. I guess it had been building for many months, maybe years, but I had no idea how it was affecting me until I found myself sobbing in my car on a dirt road near my home. Sobbing loud and uncontrollably. It was late fall of 2000, just five months after the civil union law had taken effect, and eleven months after the Supreme Court decision. Driving home from work, passing by the farms and meadows that I'd passed thousands of times before, I was jolted by the sight of one of those black and white signs mounted on the side of a barn. "Take Back Vermont" hung high so every passing motorist could see. The sight of this one felt especially assaultive. I'd always felt that farmland was friendly space and barns a soothing fit with our pastoral landscape. "Take Back Vermont" on bumper stickers and on lawn signs were bad enough—but nailed to the side of a beautiful Vermont barn, that sign screamed "Faggots not wanted here."

I was having a meltdown and I just couldn't stop crying. After more than a dozen years as an activist in the thick of the struggle for gay and lesbian equal rights, I guess I thought that my skin had toughened. I'd heard it all. Through the work for Vermont's Non-Discrimination Law in 1992 and the Adoption Reform Law in 1996, some citizens *and* legislators referred to us in the ugliest and most mean-spirited terms. It was tough, and it toughened the skin, or so I thought. And now the struggle for marriage. This had been the ugliest scene of all. Yet it had also been the most profoundly moving, as so many allies—in the Statehouse, in our neighborhoods, in our workplaces—stood for us and by us. It all hit me at once, the hatred and the humanity, on that dirt road in front of that barn near my home.

But at that moment of meltdown, something also shifted for me. And over the next few weeks, I realized that I had to try to regain what I was losing after years in the

Cheryl Gibson and Mary Hurlie have been married as life partners since 1988, and were married in civil union on July 1, 2000.

political struggle, a sense of perspective and a sense of humor. So I wrote this open letter to my fellow Vermonters, but it was really for all those who put "Take Back Vermont" signs on their lawns and barns. A version of it appeared as a letter to the editor in three area newspapers. I felt I'd rediscovered my sense of humor and was more at peace than I'd been in a long time. My partner Cheryl said she was thrilled that I'd gotten back to my old "smart-ass" self again.

December 2000

Dear fellow Vermonters:

It has been six months since Cheryl and I were joined in civil union on July 1, and I have been concerned about what detrimental effects this may have had on the marriages of my fellow Vermonters. I'm concerned about your well-being, you know; and I feel especially responsible for the crumbling state of the institution of marriage over the past half-century. So, at this six month milestone, I conducted a survey of my heterosexual friends and neighbors to determine what degree of damage my new legal status may have caused their marriage. Thought that you'd be interested in the results.

Of my heterosexual neighbors surveyed, none report deterioration in their marriage since that infamous date in July. Well, there was that one couple down the road from us who had an argument in August, but they believe that was attributable more to 90° heat and 80% humidity than it was to the new civil union law. Come to think of it, they also had quite a tiff during the heavy rain storm last month. Must be their marriage is highly weather-dependent. Anyway, the fact is, all these couples claim their marriages to be in the same state of bliss, or dysfunction, as before the date when Cheryl and I were legally joined.

Next, I polled my heterosexual colleagues at work about their home life. Each one stated that their marriages and families seemed to enjoy a rather normal stability these past six months. None of their children switched their sexual orientation during this period. Their gay kids were still gay; their straight kids were still straight. In terms of additional stress on their marital relationships, none of the respondents reported any physical symptoms of heightened stress such as tension, headaches or disorientation. Some did claim to experience intense eye strain during this past summer and fall, caused, they think, by the stark black and white signs dotting Vermont's beautiful landscape. But I believe most of them have since recovered.

Of my heterosexual married friends surveyed, all report that they are as deeply in love with each other today as they were on June 30, 2000. Several did report a physiological reaction to actually witnessing a civil union ceremony (ours), and described that reaction as something along the lines of "spine-tingling" and "heart-palpitating." None of these reactions required medical attention, however. All were treated at home with an extra dose of attention and love from their spouses.

To increase the sample size for this report, I broadened my study beyond my own circle of friends and neighbors. As a justice of the peace and officiant at over twenty civil unions to date, I've had a unique vantage on the impact that civil union ceremonies have on the mental health of heterosexual guests. Specifically, I followed the trend of observable affectional behavior of heterosexual couples immediately following their attendance at a civil union ceremony. The results here are consistent: in 100% of the cases, the subject couples exhibited a marked increase in outward physical signs of affection toward their partner. That is, more of these couples were observed hugging and holding hands with their spouses upon leaving a civil union ceremony, than were observed before the ceremony. I'm fairly certain that this behavior was then carried back with them to their homes and families.

I know that the skeptics, scientists and statisticians will be tempted to shoot holes in either my survey methodology or scientific validity of my instrumentation, so I pledge to stay on top of this issue with follow-up studies. But the evidence to date does seem to bear out what we have known all along—that the legal recognition of loving and committed relationships between women or between men most certainly does not threaten heterosexual marriage. Quite the contrary, it would seem to enlarge society's capacity for love and respect...and enrich us all.

Best regards,

Mary M. Hurlie

Mary Hurlie is a longtime activist and, since 1990, a central figure in organizing and lobbying for each of the legislative victories for gay rights in Vermont. She was a founder of the Vermont Coalition for Lesbian and Gay Rights (VCLGR). ❧

Representative Bill Lippert ~

Civil union was created through the work of many. During this process, Representative Bill Lippert, the only openly gay Vermont legislator, served as vice chair of the House Judiciary Committee. He provided strong leadership, both professionally and personally. Here are the words he addressed to the Vermont House of Representatives on March 15, 2000, as they examined several amendments put forth to defeat or diminish civil union.

I think it's important to put a face on this. I think it's important to ask who it is that we're talking about; who it is that we've been discussing. I've had the privilege in my own life of coming to the process—through a struggle at times—the process of coming to identify myself as a gay man. I've had the privilege of developing a deep, devoted, loving, caring relationship with another man. I think it's very important as we listen, as we debate and as we make decisions that you understand what the reality is about gay and lesbian people, gay and lesbian couples.

Our mailboxes have been filled with letter after letter talking about abomination, talking about sinfulness, talking about judgment day coming soon. I'm here to tell you that gay and lesbian people and gay and lesbian couples deserve not only rights, they deserve to be celebrated. Our lives, in the midst of historic prejudice and historic discrimination, are to my view, in some ways, miracles.

Think what kind of relationship you would try to establish and how successful it would be to find a loving, committed partner in an environment where you have been barraged on a daily basis, from birth, saying you are sinful or wrong, that something is fundamentally flawed in your nature. It is, in truth, the goodness of gay and lesbian people and of gay and lesbian couples that is a triumph, is a *triumph,* against discrimination and prejudice. We are not a threat. We are not a threat to

In addition to serving as state representative, Bill Lippert is the executive director of the Samara Foundation of Vermont, a lesbian and gay community foundation. Bill lives with his partner Enrique Peredo in Hinesburg, Vermont.

traditional marriage. We are not a threat to your communities. We are, in fact, an asset. We deserve to be welcomed, because in fact we are your neighbors; we are your friends; indeed, we are your family.

Numbers of people here have come up and talked to me privately about their gay brother, or lesbian sister, or their child, or their uncle. Part of those conversations are private, at times, because in fact prejudice and discrimination continue to exist in this society. Not everyone feels, even with the laws we have on our books now, not everyone feels able to say with openness and with pride, "Yes, my family member is a gay man or a lesbian woman."

We have made incredible progress in Vermont. And, up until the last two and a half months, I would have said Vermont has made more progress than any other state in this country. I have proudly said that. Our nondiscrimination laws, our hate crimes laws, our adoption laws, they all make us proud.

There remains afoot in Vermont prejudice against gay men and lesbians. In the last two and a half months I have seen it and I have heard it, I have been called names in this Chamber, in this building, the likes of which I have never experienced in my life—my personal life or my political life. And, I've watched come true what I have always known to be true, that those who stand beside gay and lesbian people as their allies, as people who are going to stand up and say, "Yes, this is wrong," and "Yes, there should be rights," they get targeted too. Because, for some people the hate runs that deep, the prejudice runs that far. I've watched while members of my committee have made brave political decisions to support equality for gay and lesbian people, for gay and lesbian couples and rights for us, and I have watched them be attacked. I have stood there and listened while they have been threatened personally and politically, and I've had members of my committee say, "I couldn't sleep at night; I've had knots in my stomach." I wouldn't have wished this on any of them, but I am deeply appreciative of the work of my committee members who listened, who struggled, came to hard reached decisions that it's the right thing to do.

Passing the bill that the House Judiciary Committee has brought forward will not end discrimination. It will not end prejudice. It will not end hate, but it will grant rights. We argue about whether they are civil rights or other rights, but I'll tell you this, they are rights that I don't have right now and most everyone else in this Chamber does. There's something strange about sitting in the midst of a deliberative body that is trying to decide whether I and my fellow gay and lesbian Vermonters should get our rights now; should we wait a little longer; should we ask all the people whether or not we deserve to have those rights.

Who are we? We are committed, caring, loving individuals in a time when desire for greater commitment, greater love, and greater fidelity is needed in our society, and I find it so ironic that rather than being embraced and welcomed, we are seen as a threat. We are people, some of us, that in recent times endured the scourge of a terrible epidemic and even in the midst of that epidemic, have reached out and formed relationships, cared for each other, holding each other, sometimes as death has arrived. Don't tell me about what a committed relationship is and isn't. I've watched my gay brothers care for each other deeply and my lesbian sisters nurse and care. There is no love and no commitment any greater than what I've seen, what I know.

Our relationships deserve every protection that our bill would grant. Our relationships deserve those rights, those protections. We don't need to study it any longer. We don't need to put it off and let someone else decide. We have a historic opportunity...to take another piece of hatred and discrimination and prejudice and remove it. At the same time, we will give an affirmation to our community about what it means to have full inclusivity, to embrace our neighbors, to affirm committed, loving relationships and to affirm our common humanity.

Thank you, Mr. Speaker.

Photograph by Karen Pike

LINDA HOLLINGDALE made her first pictures with a hand-me-down Kodak Brownie when she was nine years old. She began doing darkroom work when she was in college and continues to balance photography with her career as a personal counselor. *Creating Civil Union* is her first book, which she describes as a labor of love. Linda credits the constant support of her life partner, Mary Loney, as the sustaining force behind this project.

Mary is a registered nurse and works for the State of Vermont. Linda and Mary celebrated their wedding on September 25, 1999. They were joined in civil union on August 11, 2000.